Heed the Wisdom of the Witch

Spring would be the beginning, if there were beginnings. Spring, we fancy, comes to us once, goes once, is gone forever. But women spiral through life's seasons like the world does its own: there are days of growth in youth, in midlife, in age, just as there are losses and cold in each.

There may be a concentration of spring energies in the maiden, but she can feel as well the forces of fullness and decline. Women in their prime are maids and crones at once. And every aged woman knows still the wild spring winds. . . .

◆   ◆   ◆

About the Author

Patricia Monaghan is one of the early leaders of the contemporary goddess movement. She is a member of the resident faculty of the School for New Learning at DePaul University in Chicago, and she lectures nationally on goddess spirituality. Her poetry has been published in more than seventy magazines and journals, as well as set to music.

To Write to the Author

If you wish to contact the author or would like more information about this book, please write to the author in care of Llewellyn Worldwide and we will forward your request. Both the author and publisher appreciate hearing from you and learning of your enjoyment of this book and how it has helped you. Llewellyn Worldwide cannot guarantee that every letter written to the author can be answered, but all will be forwarded. Please write to:

Patricia Monaghan
℅ Llewellyn Worldwide
P.O. Box 64383, Dept. 0-7387-0180-7
St. Paul, MN 55164-0383, U.S.A.

Please enclose a self-addressed stamped envelope for reply, or $1.00 to cover costs. If outside U.S.A., enclose international postal reply coupon.

Many of Llewellyn's authors have websites with additional information and resources. For more information, please visit our website at:

http://www.llewellyn.com

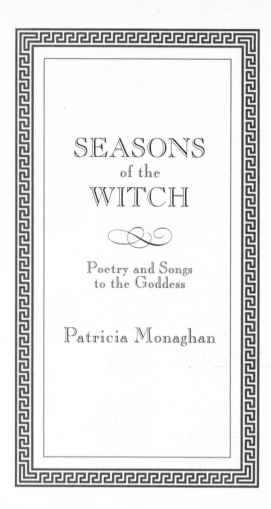

SEASONS
of the
WITCH

Poetry and Songs
to the Goddess

Patricia Monaghan

2002
Llewellyn Publications
St. Paul, Minnesota 55164-0383, U.S.A.

SECOND EDITION
First Printing, 2002

Book design and editing by Rebecca Zins
Cover design by Gavin Dayton Duffy

Library of Congress Cataloging-in-Publication Data
Monaghan, Patricia.
    Seasons of the witch : poetry and songs to the goddess /
        Patricia Monaghan.—2nd ed.
        p.   cm.
    ISBN 0-7387-0180-7
    1. Goddess religion—Poetry.   2. Seasons—Poetry.
        3. Women—Poetry.   I. Title.

PS3563.O5153 S43 2002
811'.54—dc21

2001050703

Llewellyn Publications
A Division of Llewellyn Worldwide, Ltd.
P.O. Box 64383, Dept. 0-7387-0180-7
St. Paul, MN 55164-0383, U.S.A.
www.llewellyn.com

Printed in Canada

Contents

Part One:
Grace in Action

Part Two:
Ordinary Magic

Part Three:
The Measure of Her Powers

Part Four:
To the Mountains of the Hag

Acknowledgments

Some of the poems in this book have been previously published in the following journals and anthologies:

Journals: *Green Egg, Milkweed Chronicle, Negative Capability, Plains Poetry Journal, Sing Heavenly Muse!, Visions, International Tarot Association Newsletter.*

Anthologies: *State of Peace: The Women Speak.* Natasha Borovsky, Florence Miller, Mary Rudge, and Elaine Starkman, editors. Gull Books. *With A Fly's Eye, Whale's Tale, and Woman's Heart: Animals and Women.* Theresa Corrigan and Stephanie Hoppe, editors. Cleis Press. *Return of the Goddess.* Burleigh Muten, editor. Hands of the Goddess Press. *Sleeping with Dionysus: Women, Ecstasy and Addiction.* Kay Marie Porterfield, editor. The Crossing Press. *Her Words: An Anthology of Poetry about the Great Goddess.* Burleigh Muten, editor. Shambhala Press.

Liner notes for *Drawing Down the Moon,* Rhino Records. Goddess 2000 worldwide ritual.

Preface to the Second Edition

Since this book was first published in 1992, readers have written to describe the way its poems have been woven into their lives in significant ways, by becoming part of ceremonies and rituals that mark rites of passage in individual lives and in the year's passage. One couple read a poem to mark their union under an ancient madroña tree; a women's group regularly incorporates selections in their seasonal rites; passages are copied on love notes and sympathy cards; a teacher gives sections to students to encourage their spiritual unfolding. Musicians and singers, like my sister, singer Peggy Monaghan, and Sally Coombs, Susan LaCroix, James Robbins, Claudia Blythe, Kirsten Baird Gustafson, and Lili McGovern, have heard the music behind the words and made it audible to others; some of this music has been compiled on the CD that accompanies this second edition. Nothing thrills and humbles a poet more than learning that her words have been chosen by strangers and friends as expressions of their heart's intent. I am grateful to all those who have shared with me their gratitude for the existence of these poems and their varied ways of bringing this poetry of spirit into their lives.

When asked to prepare an expanded edition, I faced the challenge of keeping the spirit of the earlier book alive while moving it into new terrain. A special problem came from the fact that, in addition to the four solar seasons that formed the most obvious organization of the earlier book, there was a hidden "lunar calendar" as well, with thirteen poems in each season recalling the months of the lunar year. In this edition, the moon's cycle is represented by the number twenty-eight, the number of poems and passages in each season. To so greatly expand the book, I have added prose poems on each of the seasonal turnings (Ostara or spring equinox; Litha, summer solstice; Mabon, fall equinox; and Yule, winter solstice) that join the earlier poems for the ancient Celtic feasts, and prose poems on the moon's major phases (crescent, full, waning, and dark). There are also several cycles of prose poems that can be read individually or as a group: the diurnal cycle (dawn, noon, evening, night), the cycle of story (beginning, complications, climax, conclusion), the agricultural cycle (planting, cultivating, harvesting, lying fallow) and the cycle of a woman's life as seen through the feminine archetypes of maiden, mother, lover, and crone.

Each season now has a song for the goddess of light, usually seen as a dancer and spoken by her male lover, for the goddess is not always alone or with other women. I have also added poems in each season that evoke my Irish/Celtic heritage; a litany for the creatures of the element associated with each season; expressions of the seasons as altars; poems inspired by cards in the major arcana of the tarot deck; and love spells in the ancient poetic form of the charm. Finally, a four-part Goddess Instruction Manual is woven through the book, its various lessons drawn from each season.

Hera, who appeared in each season in the earlier edition, is joined now by Maeve, the splendid goddess-queen of ancient Ireland, who similarly speaks in each of her multiple identities. Other goddesses appear as well, to bless and sometimes curse, each a potential aspect of our lives. Commentary on their stories is provided in the notes that follow the text. These describe the originating myth, but any readers who imagine different meanings should feel free to embrace them.

It has been an honor and pleasure to return to a book that was a milestone in my earlier spiritual and artistic life and which has become that milestone once again. I offer these poems to you with hopes that they will meet your heart's need.

◆   ◆   ◆

Warning

She won't make wigs
of it. She has more brutal plans.
Some she feeds to pigs.
Some she burns in distant lands
you never want to visit.

Is it
strange that nude
before a flat stone altar
she fashions crude
and obscene figures from your hair?
Beware
women who don't falter
when they pick up scissors or a knife,
who know the names of poison plants,
the purpose of each star,
the absolute anatomy of life.
Such women are, however,
individual and rare.
A single warning:
Never let one cut your hair.

◆   ◆   ◆

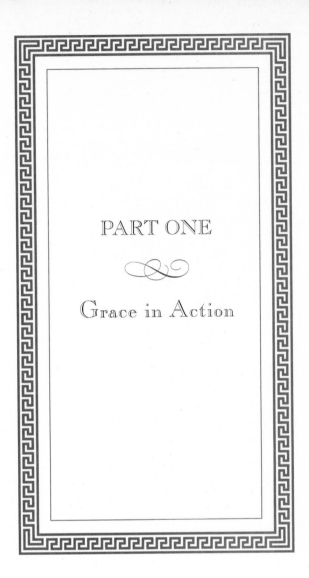

PART ONE

Grace in Action

Spring

Spring would be the beginning, if there were beginnings.

In truth, the world's seasons spiral out from one another. There can be fall in summer, winter in autumn; sudden snow can freeze the summer crop, a warm wind melt the icy river. We complain and call the weather unseasonable, but we are not surprised. We are delighted when summer floods into fall, when a fall-crisp day appears like a miracle in midwinter. But we are not surprised. We know that, in the flux of seasons, we see each one more than once.

But spring seems different. There is, sometimes in January, a springlike day when buds swell and flies' eggs hatch; there is, sometimes late in May, a winter storm to decimate the flowers. Both disturb us, disturb our springtime dream of waking into ceaseless sun and easy growth, of soft buds that flame into lasting blossoms, of graceful ease, easeful grace. Dozens of springs that creep upon us unawares, then fade imperceptibly into summer, can never convince us the season will not arrive in just one trumpet day. Spring, we fiercely believe, comes once to us and stays.

We believe as much of a woman's seasons. Spring, we fancy, comes to us once, goes once, is gone forever. But women spiral through life's seasons like the world does its own: There are days of growth in youth, in midlife, in age, just as there are losses and cold in each. There may be a concentration of spring energies in the maiden, but she can feel as well the forces of fullness and decline. Women in their prime are maids and crones at once. And every aged woman knows still the wild spring winds.

And when it comes, spring does not simply blow upon the warming air like blossom kisses. Spring is as much a time of pain as of growth. Imagine the egg, the bulb, the bud. All begin contained—all potential, endless promise. There is a quiet dignity in such presence. There is no strain, no disturbance by passion or power. The being rests within itself.

But when growth begins, things break. Shells and bud casings, those intact perfections, fall away. What is revealed is unprotected tenderness. It is no illusion, this fragility. A fierce storm can shred the new leaf, a cat consume the tiny bird, a hapless word pierce the young woman's heart.

To the beholder, there is only beauty: the frail green hue that rivals all of autumn's glory, the soft maiden gaze with its vulnerable longing. Springtime empowers its witnesses. And the woman gazing back may feel, indeed, the riveting power of her growth and potential. Or she may feel only the pain of new skin against cold wind, of exposed flesh against cruel stares.

There are times the hatchling yearns for the shell, the woman for her girlhood. There are times the new body seems alien and ill-formed, the new skills awkward and mistaken, the new knowledge not power but frailty. Growth may be exhilarating, but it is never easy.

And it is costly. Just as the bulb devours itself in order to burst above the soil, just as the hatchling digests its egg's world, the woman tears springtime out of herself. She has little time for generosity, for she is focused on herself, on her deepest movements, her pain, her hopefulness. She is all stunned inwardness.

She is one, alone, unique. She is pierced with wonder at her existence.

And from this wonder, she creates her world. It is a new world, for the world has never before been inhabited by her singular being. Her creation is a dance of wonder and power, of energy and discovery. Her dance draws the world's eye, for although she has never before lived, she lives now, and in living changes the very essence of the world.

She is each of us. We hold her within, just as we hold all seasons. Bend towards her when she sings her rasping song of growth. Honor both her pain and all her promises. And remember, too, to dance with her, for she is the power of movement and change. She is the soul within the body, the spirit flashing forth from flesh. She is the power of green life. She is the first being in the world—and she is you.

◆　　◆　　◆

Hera Renews Her Youth

Now is the time that I choose. Hermit
winter is over, my widow season.
I want lust now, endearments,
longing and song. The trees on

the hillside renew themselves
as I do. Oh, my grand thick trunk
that holds me stiff so my tassels
and catkins can fly! Oh, I'm drunk

with my greenness again! Every branch
has budded before, has flown
into leaf and then blanched
into fall. But I'm new in my bones

when I choose, I'm blood-young again,
I rise fresh as washed granite
from foam, I love whom and when
I choose. Here I stand, pomegranate

in hand, ripe as a bud but old, old
as rock, unshakeable now, a power
essentially female and free. Hold
my ripe breasts. I'll be gone in an hour.

◆　◆　◆

The Goddess Instruction Manual,
Part One: How to Think like Athena

1. Remove shoes.
Stand on earth.

2. Find your center.
Find your balance.

3. Lift chest. Drop shoulders.
Let palms fall open at sides.

4. Open lips. Breathe.
Feel air pass into self.

5. Open eyes wide.
Look to the horizon.

6. Ask, what says the foot?
Ask, what says the leg?

7. Ask, what says the sex?
Ask, what says the heart?

8. Ask, what sees the eye?
Ask, what hears the ear?

9. The mind is the body.
Think everywhere at once.

◆ ◆ ◆

Planting

Potential, they call it. Youth, they say, is full of potential. Spring, full of potential.

It sounds so hopeful. As though potential always means growth and bursting life, extravagant boom, fullness of fruit.

I am in the garden in soft rain. Dark soil clings to my skin. Rain slides down my neck like tears. My hair curls against temples and neck, tendrils in rain. The moon is new. It is time for planting.

From my pocket I take a white packet from which I pour a hundred seeds, tiny seeds that barely fill my palm. Into chevrons my hoe has grooved into the soil, I slowly pour these weightless bits of life. In a few weeks dark reddish green will appear. In a few months, those leaves will become my food. In a season, the plants will grow and die, as in my season I grow and will die.

Not all these seeds will sprout. Some will not survive the tearing open of their protective casing. Some will never raise shoulders, then heads, to the sun. Some will be tattered by hard rain, some betrayed by hail, some eaten by insects and birds, some thinned by my gardener's hand.

Potential: for death, for failure, as surely as for life and success.

So it is with me: Some selves that might have flowered were stillborn, some happinesses died in the struggle to endure, some talents never fruited. It is easy to grow hard, as though by failing to hope we can avoid inevitable pain. But plant a hundred seeds, and ten will grow. Plant ten, and one will grow. There is no reason not to be profligate with seed, as with hope.

So every season of my life I plant, and plant, and plant again. I do not stint on seed, those tiny miracles, those small promises. For some things survive. Some things endure. And that must be enough.

◆　◆　◆

Maia, Grandmother Spring

She throws the covers off
and bares herself: dirty

leaves, dry gray bodies
of last year's grasses,

trees felled by snow,
mangled branches.

Then she turns over
in her muddy bed and

rises slowly, slowly:
bulbs burgeon into

chalices and trumpets,
redbirds pipe and court,

buds fur the empty
twigs, leaves unfurl.

The air is moist with
rot and growth, she is

all mud and death,
daughter, grandmother,

freedom and escape, how
did we forget (how we will

forget again, so soon, so soon)
this loss, these promises?

♦   ♦   ♦

Wild Sound

Yours are the hands
of a magician
of wildernesses:

like iris transmuted
into wild blue flags
what you touch escapes
from cultivation instantly
like roses collapsing
into fruitfulness—

You touch me and
suddenly lawns grow
rampant with bedstraw.
A fieldstone path dissolves
into a canyon. Cedars crush
an ornamental hedge.

An ancient order reasserts
itself, and this, from your
one charm: you know
no garden long withstands
the sorcery of freedom.

Some things change quickly.
Farther north, the slow
responses: glaciers stir.
Migrations swell like canticles.
And the locked sea opens
to the seeking whale
its savage revelations.

◆　◆　◆

She Who Watches and Holds Still

From the top of the round tower
a naked woman looked down
upon the darkening road north.

Whirlwinds blew across the road,
little vortices of wind and sand.
She held her arms up to the sky.

The white sky tilted towards blue.
Horsemen appeared, riding steadily.
She watched with no fear, no fury.

She stood there fearless as the star fell
high above the tower. She stood there
as the wind rushed up the tower wall.

Now she is sleeping on the parapet,
the winds still and calm, the riders encamped,
the stars holding their places in the sky.

◆   ◆   ◆

Altar of the East

in a clear vase, one bud
a thin and dawn-pink ribbon

a cone of dark incense
from the farthest desert

a white candle
the picture of a child

a single feather
a flute carved of reed

a magnifying glass
a scroll, inscribed by hand

a stoppered silver bottle
containing just your breath

◆　◆　◆

Aubade for Aurora: Her Lover Sings to the Dawn Goddess

I sleep beside a winding stream,
unarmored, naked as the night.
I sleep near water far from dawn.

The stream stirs in its stony bed.
I hear its music as I wake.
The woods are dark so far from dawn.

I slip into the sweet warm stream,
swim gently first, then plunge and dive,
in love with water, far from dawn.

And then I rest all wet and spent
on the warm grass of a garden full
of shadowed roses far from dawn.

O goddess, dearest, follow me
for dark and fragrant secrets hide
wherever lovers outwit the dawn.

Only your water quenches my thirst.
Only your water cools my brow.
Small birds are calling now to dawn,

but close your gray eyes, love, and sleep
here on the ground, tight in my arms,
for a closed eye can see no dawn.

There is no sun above us can match
the silver light of your body in love.
Let us hide in that light, my lady, for dawn

sounds a faint echo of you—but you rise.
Mere daylight fills your gray eyes.
All dims. The garden dissolves. This dawn

has no light. You leave—then you turn.
My parched heart springs hopeful again.
But it's only a glance—then you walk into dawn.

♦　♦　♦

Dawn

A bird is singing.

From a deep dream I hear it, embroidering the air in loops and swirls. I am swimming deep within myself, swimming upwards to a bright blue sheet on which a yellow circle shines. I break the surface into thin bright light.

A bird is singing.

Its song is sharp and bright as its red feathers. Each morning it perches in the maple outside my room to greet the dawn, to sing up the sun. Slowly the light grows warmer, more golden.

The ancients, in the courtesy of great need, bowed to the rising sun. The solo bird, too, greets her eminence as she ascends the sky. Soon the dawn chorus begins, a great swell of chittering and whistling and trumpeting.

Light and sound. Light and sound.

For a few moments, they are one.

My own dawn song is wordless, soundless, the stirring of a great ocean of gratitude within me. I leap like a dancer from my dream. And then, with a light heart, I open my arms to the great gift of day.

◆　◆　◆

Litany of Air

Red-breasted robin,
> *great golden eagle,*

nuthatch and vireo,
> *condor and seagull,*

barn owl and peregrine,
> *penguin and ptarmagin,*

swallow and oriole,
> *trumpeter swan.*

Pigeon and peacock,
> *great golden eagle,*

Bluejay and heron,
> *condor and seagull,*

Cardinal, woodcock,
> *penguin and ptarmagin,*

Snow bunting, loon,
> *trumpeter swan.*

Woodpecker, titmouse,
> *great golden eagle,*

Pelican, kestrel,
> *condor and seagull.*

Raven and ibis,
> *penguin and ptarmagin,*

Pheasant and sawbill,
> *trumpeter swan.*

Migrating mallard,
　　great golden eagle,
Bobolink, kittiwake,
　　condor and seagull,
Quail, crow, and parrot,
　　penguin and ptarmagin,
Goldfinch and corncrake,
　　trumpeter swan.

♦　♦　♦

Venus of Lespugue

I remember a calm world,
weatherless under a white sky,
a sky unserrated by stars,
with a round unmoving sun.

I was safe, contained, secure.
I floated calmly in the world.
I needed nothing. I never moved.
I watched my own red heart.

Then, in a twist, a spasm, a gasp,
I felt desire: My body pulsed
sharply with longing, I felt
my blood seethe, my loins melt,

and I wanted, all at once,
to burst from that sunshine
bliss, I wanted all at once
to fly out into chaos,

I wanted to leave the pure
world shattered behind,
I wanted to rise from that shell
like an angel, like a new sprout.

I lifted my arms and raged
against the ruins of my shell,
against the ruin of my shell.
I lifted myself from myself.

I arched forth like a seed
dissolving itself in growth,
like a bird breaking
out of itself in growth.

And as I moved I felt
the blast of a new sun on
my opening wings, a new
wind on my opening leaves.

♦   ♦   ♦

Swan Maiden

As I stand here before you
you do not see me, not really,

for I have another body,
my real self, stronger, sleeker

than this clumsy rough
flesh, this prison of longing.

In that other body I float
across water like a blossom,

I float across the sky like
a star transforming itself.

You are to blame for this. Hidden
in damp grass by a midnight lake,

you found and stole my swanskin robe.
You crippled me. Without it, I am all

nakedness and pain. Without it
I stand before you flightless, weeping.

Somewhere in a dim dusty box
in a darkened cellar are my wings,

my feathered hood. Somewhere
are all my stolen beauties,

that rainbow arc of flight,
that floating circle of grace.

Though I stand here before you,
you do not remember who I am:

a swan trumpeting from the wild
skies, an archangel of spring.

◆   ◆   ◆

Finola's Song

The gorse is blooming again,
and wild rhododendron.
Roses bud in the rain,
always and never the same.
Above, the wild geese skein.

Once I kept count of the years.
The sky would cloud and clear,
the sun rise, shine, and disappear,
while I, the daughter of Lir,
counted each hour, each tear.

The gorse is blooming again,
and wild rhododendron.
Roses bud in the rain,
always and never the same.
Above, the wild geese skein.

A century passed, and another.
I believed that I should number
each moment since my brothers
and I lost ourselves and our father,
both in the wave of a feather.

The gorse is blooming again,
and wild rhododendron.
Roses bud in the rain,
always and never the same.
Above, the wild geese skein.

I thought it my task to remember.
But one spring, as I stared at a flower
in its frail momentary power,
I forgot to make note of the hour
and fell into timeless wonder.

The gorse is blooming again,
and wild rhododendron.
Roses bud in the rain,
always and never the same.
Above, the wild geese skein.

Love is not fooled by a mask.
We float on oceans of glass,
and endure the storm's blast, its blast,
and the days pass, the days pass,
unnumbered, uncounted, at last.

♦   ♦   ♦

The Fool

Here you are again, turning up
just when I'm trying to pretend
everything's under control,

your cap so jaunty, your little dog
frisking at your feet, that flower
in your hand, your chin high,

and the sun, the sun so vibrant
whenever you appear, turning
the whole sky yellow with liquid light,

and the mountains seem to melt
into meringue, their ice seems
suddenly froth, and even the rocks

are like gingerbread, everything seems
fanciful and sweet, and even though I know
you are standing above an abyss

into which you could so readily tumble—
rose, jaunty hat, little dog, high boots and all—
and though I see all the dangers in this prospect,

you delight me, Fool, I call out a greeting
more in joy than in warning, and you
seem for just a moment to turn your head—

♦   ♦   ♦

Nimue's Charm for Finding Love

Sun and moon, attend to me:
Be my eyes, my restless eyes.
Show me where my love lies.

Wind and air, attend to me:
Be my breath, my searching words.
Whisper sweetness to my love.

Ocean, rivers, rain, attend:
Let all water taste of me.
Let my love grow thirsty, thirsty.

Now earth, great force, attend, attend:
Be my flesh, my heart, my skin.
Touch my love everywhere. Begin!

Elements and elementals, come:
I am alone. The world is wide.
Bring my lover to my side.

◆   ◆   ◆

Crescent Moon

After darkness, such radiance.

A gentle curve: slender, deep, serene. Just at sunset, just before dawn, dancing on the horizon like a promise. And in the deep of night, cresting the sky like a woman in flight.

I gather offerings: a small rose crystal, a tiny coin, a seed. I place them in the eastern window. I lift my hands, palms to face, and gaze across the night at her, riding so there gracefully, a sliver of possibility.

All month I await this opening, this seeding moment. Look, I whisper. Look what I have brought. Look. Look here.

In silver light I cast my hope on the wide sea of night. In a sliver of light I open myself to possibility.

Light shimmers down.

Does she see? Does she see?

◆　◆　◆

Diana to Her Maiden

No, sapling, no, I cannot climb
you yet, you bend in each
breeze like a flame in wind,

it is too soon, too soon.
Next year we will go
hunting under the half moon

and fall, damp and breathless
on soft moss near a stream,
and I will sing yes, yes,

the time and you are ripe, sapling,
little tree, and I will climb,
then, climb your brown limbs

and we will be all sugared
from the sap of you then,
the two of us tangled, ungirded,

unguarded, unblushing, unbound.
Oh, girl, your soft limbs . . .
Go, go call the hounds.

♦   ♦   ♦

Ostara

For a moment, she is still. Like a dancer or an acrobat, she who is always in motion pauses, balanced perfectly, beautifully at rest for the space of a breath. Everything is complete: All her movements, graceful and exact, have led to this instant where she stands poised like a small bird on the brink of flight, like a spring branch at the cusp of leafing, like a large-eyed doe at meadow's edge.

Then, before we can applaud, she is moving again, flinging herself headlong into time and action. For it is not her way to hold still, she who is movement itself. Except for these poignant perfect moments when we see her like a statue of glass or ebony or marble. Except for these instants where the earth rests for a moment so that we may take in our breath, once, sharply, in awe of her beauty and magnificence.

And then she is moving again. We are moving again. The world is moving again.

Balance is not stasis but action. Not immobility but gesture. Not inertia but flux.

The moment between two movements. The pause between two pulses.

The pause . . .

For a moment, she is still. Then the dancer bends and sways. The acrobat leaps free. The bird lifts from its branch into the warming air, the branch unfolds its tender green, the doe springs back into the dark forest.

How can we say the cycle begins anew? It never ended.

♦   ♦   ♦

Atalanta to Her Father

my love must be like
the birch groves
where I run
like moss that spreads
under me and springs
up as I pass so
will I yield to
the right lover

oh I love

the sky as I run the sky
against my chest the wind
when I run everywhere
there are flowers and
in winter everywhere
are promises

I do not want
so much, I want
someone I can-
not outrun

why should I not
stretch and spring
my mind my
heart my legs

stronger
why not
swifter
why

should I
ever be
bounded
bound—

the mind leaps
like a deer—

why should I
not be free

◆　　◆　　◆

Maiden

It is so easy to forget the rawness of her rage.

She is young, and sweet as all young things are, tender in her own way, soft and yielding when she chooses, playful and winsome. She is a puppy or a fawn, she is coltish and kittenish, she's a vixen, an eaglet, a lion's cub.

And it is so easy to forget the rawness of her rage.

In the forest, the maiden goddess lives, wild and strong. She surrounds herself with other maidens who run barefoot and barebreasted, swift and free, alongside her. With them run lean hunting hounds, baying in full-blooded excitement. When they grow tired of the chase, the maidens plunge into cool shaded pools, where they dart about like minnows in silver water. Their bodies sleek and silver, they rest briefly upon the shore. Then the hounds bay again and, leaping up, the maidens set off once more. They are strong and vibrant. Power pulses through them like joy, like life.

They are so beautiful, it is easy to forget the rawness of their rage.

Some of us enter the sacred forest with eyes closed to its beauty. Some enter the forest hurt, intending to hurt in return. Some enter in arrogance, refusing to bow to anything but their own corrupted will. For these, the maiden's beauty is a challenge or an insult, something to be destroyed or possessed.

And thus they encounter the rawness of her rage.

She is the conscience of our race, this fury who protects the sacredness of Earth, whose lean dogs fly at the throats of those who would profane the beauty she holds dear. She is mighty in her rage, knowing justice and its absence, knowing respect for life and its absence, knowing spirited love and its absence. She rages inside each of us, commanding us to live freely in the present, in ways that nurture the future.

The maiden's arrow is swift and sharp and true. She herself is swift and sharp and true. Ignore her at your peril.

◆　◆　◆

Persephone's Invitation

Let us go and lie together
in a field of new grasses
under the honey sun.

Let us lie like twins
with each other, trace
each other's faces, braid

each other's hair, let us
compare desires, reveal
the shapes of all our dreams,

and let us whisper secrets:
how hills rise up from
meadows, how warm rivers

overflow their curving banks,
how flowers burst into
bloom beneath our fingers.

You are a flower yourself,
lady, petaled with life
and fragrant with promises.

Let me write in secret
alphabets all that I know
upon your tender skin.

Let me hide my face
against your soft neck
and feel time stop,

feel spring become
eternal under your
gaze, your touch, feel

the bitter future retreat
beneath the earth in his
brassy clanging chariot.

◆   ◆   ◆

Persephone's Journey

I lay at rest in the violet-fragrant
meadow, that other world
of honey sun and maiden beauty,
nothing moving, nothing moving
except the bees penetrating
the blossoms near my hand,
except the catkins swaying
in the wind-touched willow,
except the sparrows, the sparrows
with their bright dancing song.

That was my world then:
Peace, I thought, perfection,
yes, perfection, the sun warm
against my skin and the breezes
in my hair and the sap rising
in the red-gold dogwood, in
the red linden, in the willow thicket.

The sap was rising in me
too. I did not know it, I did not
know that I was waiting, waiting,
coiled like a snake or a fern's frond,
curled tight against myself, ready
to shed myself, ready to unfurl,
ready—

He arrived like an earthquake.
He arrived like a storm
on spring leaves. He arrived like
a great hawk from a vacant sky.
He arrived like an antlered
deer by a waterfall. He arrived
like a wolf from the hills.

I felt myself break apart.
I felt like a continent set loose
to drift upon the ocean. I felt
like a comet in cold space.
I felt like the first horse,
the first horsewoman.
I felt like new fire.

My soul flew out through my eyes
like a tiny bird, my soul flew out
through my eyes like a butterfly.

The world disappeared.
Yes, the world disappeared.
And I did not care.

He led me to a place
that I had seen in dreams,
a place where blue
winds ripped across
cold mountain passes
and tiny asters
starred from gray rock
and the universe flowed
and flowered and flamed.

He took me to places silent
and precise, pastures where
grass rippled like muscle,
where bees alit on flowers
still as carvings, where
impermanence was graven
into time and flesh became
stone, became crystal, became
star's metal, became obsidian.

I became transformed.
My hands became eyes.
My eyes became hands.
My breasts became mouths.
My mouth became a beast,
a ravening beast, a famished
and ravishing beast.

He was an eagle above me,
a whale beneath me, he was
a distant asteroid, he was
alien and beautiful.
I breathed in his difference
like violet flowers.
I bathed in his difference
as in the oil of almonds.

And so I took his seed.
I took it inside me.
And not just once.

He was a pomegranate,
all leathery ripe flesh,
and I took every seed,
every red kernel,
every fragment of him.
I could not stop.
I would not stop.
I did not stop.

And then I left him.

I left him because I remembered
meadows where eyes did not peer
from every leaf. I remembered hills

where the hands of trees did not
stroke me as I passed. I remembered
solitude. I remembered myself.

I remembered a wild northern
lake in spring. I remembered it
in my blood, in my mouth.

It had been easy to go with him.
It was not easy to leave. The world
seemed dry and cold. The world

seemed empty. But I walked
away from his fire and
his knowledge, into my own.

I walked until I saw sharp peaks
and sheep climbing on sharp
hooves into slanting sunlight.

I walked until I saw an eagle rise
from a dead tree beside a river
that braided itself into a lake.

I passed the tracks of a silver fox.
I passed the muddy tracks of a bear.
I passed the silent hidden grouse.

I knew in my heart, in my blood,
of a wide pass between two
rocky peaks. I needed no map.

I heard ghosts singing in the box
canyon. I heard their secret names.
I whispered them to the deep rocks.

I knew the hunger of all beasts
and the blood-taste of food. I knew
there was purpose in all movement.

I moved towards the windy pass.
And as I reached it, day and night
swung into equipoise. The planet

tilted into perfect balance. And I began
to dance, solitary and strong,
on the moving rim of the world.

◆　◆　◆

Fand Calls the Wild Hunt

Come be free with me
in the deep groves,

come be free with me
on the mountainside.

Build me a fire
under the bright moon

and lift your arms
and voice to me,

drum with your heart,
with your dancing feet,

dance wild, more
wild, sap rising up

in you, sap rising up
in the trees that circle

you, in the grass that
bends under you, wild—

Stamp like horses, toss
your heads like mares,

bay like wolves and
roar, lionesses, roar.

Mount the sky with me
on birds, on deer, ride

with me down the valleys,
ride wild and free, ride

the pulsing night, ride
the winds of dawn,

ride wild with me,
ride wild with me.

◆   ◆   ◆

Maenad in Spring

days ago power
rose in the birch grove
now the white limbs grow
thicker with sap

wrap up in ribbons
dance through the forest
move in procession
sing shout and clap

press to the trunk now
draw out the sugar
feel the blood answer
wild in your thighs

fire on hilltops
oh the spring dances
taste of sweet syrup
feel the sap rise

    ◆   ◆   ◆

Maeve Prepares for Beltane

Before anyone praises me,
I must praise myself.

>My flaming hair.
>My noble nose.
>My brilliant eyes.

Before anyone desires me,
I must feel my own desire.

>My full soft lips.
>My swan neck.
>My full soft breasts.

Before anyone knows me,
I must know myself.

>My polished skin.
>My round belly.
>My welcoming thighs.

Before anyone loves me,
I must fully love myself.

>My briar patch.
>My secret rose.
>My fierce heart.

Before the fires blaze,
I set myself alight.

◆　　◆　　◆

On Mayday Eve

This is dead center
of the greening season.
As shadows lengthen
we drink sweet wine.

There is a moment yet this
side of the veil. Let me hold
your hand and feel the course
of suns and seasons upon us.

Sit here with me for just
a moment longer. Let me
seek within your eyes shadows
of the lengthening shadows.

I know already the body you
will put on tonight, the head
that of a deer, the flanks those
of oxen, the wings of hawks.

And I know the body I will
wear, the gliding wings and
dark beak, the lion mane,
the lidless ocean eyes.

Our minds will soon
dissolve into our limbs,
our words become all
movement and grace.

We will be changed by what
passes between us this pivot
night, this moment poised
between sap and leaf,

between bud and flower.
We will never again be
what we are now. We will
be more. We will be less.

Let us sit for another moment
before the dancing, finding
in each other's eyes shadows
of the lengthening shadows.

◆   ◆   ◆

The Beginning

You can start anywhere.

But the opposite is also true: You must start somewhere.

Shall we call birth the beginning? Or conception? The moment when electricity arched for the first time between the parents? The parents' own births, conceptions? Their own parents' meeting?

A beginning defines the story.

But beginnings are always a matter of choice. Perhaps our only real choice in the telling of our lives: to decide where to begin.

What has brought you to this moment? Can you trace back far enough to know?

Every story has an infinite number of possible beginnings. And the opposite is also true: Every moment, every instant, is a seedbed from which innumerable stories flower.

This moment, as you recite these words, is the beginning of everything that will follow. Everything.

And it is also an ending of all that has gone before. As is every moment. Turning and turning, beginning and ending, until we say, "There. Stop there. I say there. That is where it begins."

And when we speak, as we speak, it begins.

◆　◆　◆

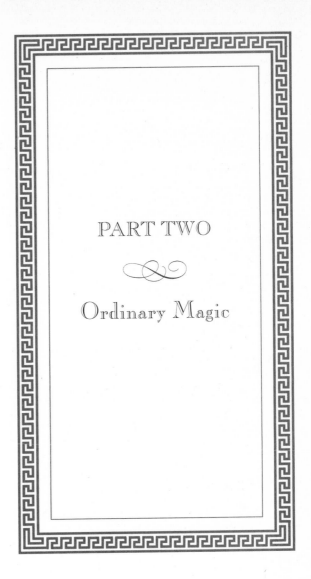

PART TWO

Ordinary Magic

Summer

Let us go out to the garden to understand.

Look: Everything is full, fleshed out. A few months ago, plants stood small and separate in the brown earth. Now leaves press, rows crowd, into each other. Summer is a season that seems but a moment. Everything seems to happen at once. Everything seems on the verge: Peaches redden, corn tassels. Tomatoes fill the air with acridity, roses with heady spice. The sun is high and hot, the days long and ripe.

This is the season of urgency. There is never enough time. Everything must be done now. This is the season of too muchness: too many blackberries, too much zucchini, too many tomatoes. It is a time of dense sensuality. The air is syrupy on humid nights as peaches poach on the stove and steaming glass jars wait. The air is cool on the porch where breezes sway the vines as a stately full moon rises. It is the season of gifts: potlucks and fairs, baskets of overripe fruit, extra produce brought to friends' homes.

Nature is in a splendor of excess. Even the garden's villains are excessive: the starling flock taunting from the apricot tree, the myriad crawling pests, the slugs creeping through evening's cool. The weather, too, is excessive. This is the time of violent winds that tear apart the harvest. Of sheeting rain that shreds and drowns. Of drought and failure: corn desiccated on the stalks, soil blowing in fierce grit winds.

Summer is bountiful. Summer is extreme. Earth is not kind nor gentle, save on those pale nights when even the sky holds still for a moment and, through the hush of a sleeping world, the heartbeat of time is heard.

So, too, for women, the summer of life. She is in her prime, full of energy. Life is endless, endlessly crowded. It draws her here, there, here, with new desires and demands. Every sunrise is an opportunity, every noon a driving compulsion, every sunset a dawn into night's possibilities. She is full and brash and busy. She takes and discards lovers; she produces children and art; she creates a self and a home. She is exhilarated by her power, exhausted by possibility. She says yes to everything, everything grows and burgeons from her energy, she is a forcefield of affirmation.

But this is also the time of losses so huge they seem to stretch to the horizon: parents gone, children in pain, the world convulsed with war. Tornadoes of feeling sweep through her, this woman in summer years. Sometimes she feels a vast hunger, an enormous yearning, as though her soul can never be sated. Sometimes she feels as though beauty is a thin membrane stretched over pain. In the midst of excess, she feels wrenching want, for there is never enough: enough time, enough tears, enough love.

Summer comes to women more than once. It opens, a wave of green energy, driving us to productiveness and passion. Summer can explode upon a woman at any time, whenever the force of life rages through her, whenever life's ache opens her eyes to the magic and beauty in each moment.

The magic of the season rests in transformation: seed into fruit, embryo into child, idea into reality. Daily the magic occurs, so fast we fail to see it. But within this flux of transformation, there are moments of perfect stillness: a hawk pivots perfectly in a tight sky circle, a star glows a single second before falling. Inside those moments, power lives. Power that is beyond the normal magic of growth and death. In these moments, time can reverse itself, all forms may change, all directions flow into their opposites. This is the secret of witches and initiates: to recognize these moments and, falling into the vast space behind them, become timeless and free. Go into the garden for understanding. Let power flow through you. Touch yourself. Touch each other. Transformation rests within you and among you. You are always transforming yourself. Just watch. Just watch.

◆   ◆   ◆

Hera Celebrates Her Ripeness

I am, at this moment, perfect.
    I am at my fullest time.
I am an apple, ripe, unpicked.
    I am the apple wine.

I am at my fullest time.
    Spring has passed, winter's ahead.
I am drunk on apple wine.
    Come into my bed.

Spring has passed, winter's ahead.
    This is my peak, my height, my best.
Come be wanton in my bed.
    Welcome to the harvest.

This is my peak, my height, my best.
    I am an apple, ripe, unpicked.
Welcome. Taste the fruits of harvest.
    I am full now. I am perfect.

◆   ◆   ◆

Full Moon

Near the river, wolves are howling.

On the hill, I stand watching. Across the valley, the moon rides on low clouds, a queen in her chariot. She who pulls the ocean's tides has pulled me from the dark comfort of my home to this circle of silver light.

From my bed, I felt her rise. I come in answer to her silent call.

I cannot sleep. Nothing sleeps when she calls. In the forest, the scuttle of mice and voles. The clattering steps of moose. The great whirring wingbeat of a hawk. Nothing can be still in the presence of her majesty.

Wolves call to each other. Coyotes sing. Spruce dances in the wind.

Unable to remain silent in her presence, I hum a simple wordless song. Soon I am shouting to the forest and the wolves and the moon.

I raise my arms and swing them, arms wide. I whirl and whirl and whirl, tracing her circular face on the silvered ground beneath me.

Singing and whirling, whirling and singing, I become the trees, the wolves, the hillside, the clouds, the mountains, the dark sky, the hunting hawk. I become the song, the dance, the words, the tune, the movement.

Above our celebration, she glides on, pale queenly moon, as the tides and the wolves and the women follow.

♦　♦　♦

Deirdre's Pledge to Her Lover

The full moon above a blossoming tree
at midnight. The sun opening a red road
across a silver lake. A giant sleeping
in the blue-gray hills. A crane, calling
from an island's shadow side.
A holy well in high summer.
The secret names of rivers.

These are the gifts you offered me,
laying them before me one by one,
more precious than jewels,
more valuable than cattle,
the finest dowry you could offer,
though you did not have to bring me
anything but yourself, your dear sweet self,
that otter playfulness and stag power
and stone strength, that great open heart,
I need no gift beyond your body
next to mine, your mouth on mine,
the dark groans of your pleasure
in the wild still night.

To one who brings such richness,
what can I offer in return?
I have only a sackful of words,
old words polished with use

and time and change.
From that sack I pull out
some for you:

Granite. Oracle. Fire.
Charm. Star. Flood.

I press them into your hands
like gifts, like promises.
Turn each one over like a jewel.
Find its hidden face, its secret facets.
Let each one etch itself upon your bones
as they have etched themselves on mine,
so that centuries from now they can still be read,

so that when our bones are found
a millennium hence, this night
will still be written on them
in the ogham of the heart:

Steady as granite is my love for you,
my oracle of happiness, you who have
come from the past bearing all my future;
I am wildfire when you press
charmed hands upon me; here is
my heart, offered in a flood of stars.
Here, my charming one, is the oracle
I write in granite for you: flooded with love,

we sleep together in a fire circle under ancient stars.
There is nothing more lasting than my love
for you, not granite nor the oldest star; no charm
more magical than your love flooding
over me, O my oracle of fire.

Arrange them as you will, these words will say
forever what I say tonight to you in words
that seem as newas dawn, as old as stone:

Here is my heart, my hand,
my mind, my body, soul and spirit.
All I ever wanted
you have brought to me.
All I have to give is yours.

◆   ◆   ◆

Instructions

Let us go walking beyond the pool
down the gravel paths to the moon.

Let us walk without talking until
we find, somewhere in the forest,

a small clearing where
moonlight falls like snow.

Take my face between your hands, then.
Kiss me. That will be enough to make

grass grow thick beneath our feet,
the crickets sing suddenly—enough,

in the pleated sky, to make
one star lose its hold and fall.

◆   ◆   ◆

Cultivating

It is hot, so hot. Sweat runs down my sides, my back, my brow. So hot.

My arms ache. My hands are black with soil.

There is never enough time. Too many tasks: one more, one more, one more again.

Crabgrass creeps beneath the cucumbers. The onion patch sprouts pigweed. Parsley and clover twine about each other.

I am thinning carrots when the rain starts. Just a trickle. I do not stop. More rain. My back, already wet with sweat, is wet again, and cool. My hair sticks to my face. When I push it away, a streak of black soil. I continue. So much to do. Not enough time.

The tomatoes have escaped their cages. I tie them up, supporting green, near-ripe globes. The potatoes need more dirt. The rain has stopped. I did not even notice when.

Hours pass. Prune. Transplant. Divide. Weed. Mulch.

It grows dark. I sit, watching fireflies flash in code. The corn pulses with growth. A raccoon creeps towards the tomatoes. Tomorrow—

◆   ◆   ◆

Dame Gothel's Love for Rapunzel

My old arms were red. The fences
for the snow peas to tear down
were up. The potatoes churned,
restless in their sandy beds.

Suddenly you were in my garden,
not a perennial I could set
among rocks, a happy place
for sprawlers, but some rare

mushroom that lifts fleshy
flowers only when rain
falls in heavy sheets
on certain crucial days.

I grew so profligate with seed
that I cannot remember where
I planted the dill. Your body
is as dizzying as sunshine.

I take a stale sweet bundle
made of stalks of last year's herbs
and bury it near the carrots,
chanting to the old red soil:

Let summer be good.
Let life be full.
Let her come home to me.
Let her come home.

✦   ✦   ✦

Complications

Once ended, stories are so easy to name.

What a comedy, we smile. Or, such a tragedy, as we wipe our tears. From the peak of meaning, we understand how each action led inevitably, inexorably, to the next.

But in the middle, we cannot see so clearly. Each instant graphs endless intersections of innumerable lines. We move each moment through a storm of possibilities, surrounded by others around whom other possibilities storm.

At times the story's shape seems clear. We understand— we imagine that we understand—the pattern. We know—we think we know—where the path is leading. But everything can change in an instant.

We cannot know the shape until the story ends.

Great promise can end in misery. Great sorrow can be lifted into greater joy. The end defines the story.

And so we stand in the storm of possibilities, wet to the core but dancing with each other whenever we can, singing as gaily as we can, "And so it goes, and so it goes."

◆　◆　◆

The Goddess Instruction Manual, Part Two: How to Act like a Maenad

1. First, sort need from want.
Then notice what invites
your taking. Steal it.

2. Close your eyes.
Throw back your head.
Listen to your pulse.

3. Drink mountains.
Eat the wind.
Dance with everything.

4. Find companions.
Do not mistake them
for partners.

5 Allow sufficient time.
The world does not break
open in an hour.

6. At the entrance, dance.
As you enter, dance.
After entering, dance.

7. Everything intoxicates.
Everything is intoxicated.
You, intoxicated, are everything.

8. You will know when you know.
You will not know until then.
Keep the secret.

◆　◆　◆

The Maps of Magic

The magic places? Listen:
the old oak at the third
crossroad creaks loudest
of any in the county.

Do not expect me to betray
what lives beyond it nor
which of the paths to take.
Trust your eyes to grow clear
and dim and clear again.
Trust too the birches,
their loudness, and do not
neglect to bring them
offerings, things coveted
among trees, a piece of sky,
a broken ruby, your cut hair—

I talk too much. I do not
know what I am saying.
A bee told me all this
and now a swarm is rising
slowly across the field,
rasping a warning.

◆   ◆   ◆

The Forest Rules

Think of it as a kind of

speech: mushrooms shake
their heads when you stoop
to pick them. Berries drift
away on a sudden breeze. These
are not yet to be eaten. And the dead

disdainful tree is not yet
to be cut, no matter
how long it has stood easy
against the air, ready to

fall. And when it does, it may
still refuse you, until one day
it is ready, silent as fuel,
empty of the speech that filled
your eyes. Of course

none of this happens
but it does not happen
exactly like this.

◆   ◆   ◆

Wisdom of Elders

the thin thirsty
tree croaks for
water

as it does
a duck flies
into view—

a fish leaps
into the duck's
mouth, becomes

a water tree, glossy
bark stream-
ing branches—

yes birds and
fish spawn forests,
rivers—the trees

wish to speak in
the constant silver
of streams,

not just stand to be
spoken through—
the trees wish me

to tell you this

◆   ◆   ◆

Litha

She had been climbing, climbing. She had reached the place beyond which is nothing but sky and descent.

At the summit, no fanfare, no balloons, no celebration. One step like all the other steps, and she was there. One more step, and the descent would begin.

As she climbed, she did not think of the summit. She watched her hands, her feet, her balance, as she rose high, high, higher.

Suddenly, she had taken the last upward step.

Do you think she made camp and slept? Do you think she stopped moving? Do you think she lives there still, at the height she sought and won?

No. What would life be without movement, without struggle? How can a clutched hand hold freedom?

She stood for a moment, entranced with the beauty of the world beneath her feet.

Then she took another step.

◆　◆　◆

Mother

Ma. Mama. Mommy. Mom. Mam.

No separation. Even in sleep, she is pressed by them, presses them, impresses them, heart and mind filled as body was once filled. Even in sleep, she fills us, knows us, senses us, our needs, our desires, our demands.

Ma. Mama. Mommy. Mom. Mam.

Never alone. Someone always tugging, at sleeve, at heart, at patience. No separation.

Mommy. Mommy. Ma, ma, ma.

She dances, she sings, she is beautiful in her desire. But even in that dance, that song, even that desire, even then she is plural: another, others, always with her, within her, she never without. And we, never without her.

Ma. Mammy. Mommy. Mom.

Always the need, hurt, demand. Always the fullness. The press, the plurality. Always someone tugging. Never alone.

Ma. Mama. Mommy.

Feeling need as it rises. At a cry, milk comes. At a sob, arms stretch. Like bursting, to hold back. She floods, she reaches, she holds, she touches, she touches, she touches. She becomes us; we become her; no separation. Need answering need answering need.

Mammy. Mommy. Mom.

Matter, *mater*, material, materialize. Flesh of woman. This our body, this our blood. Never alone. No separation.

Ma. Ma.

The open mouth. The full breast. The surge of connection.

The matrix: core of being.

Ma.

◆　◆　◆

Venus of Willendorf

Once I ate your flesh, mother.
Once I drank your blood.

That was the time of no hunger.
That was the time of no thirst.

Your cannibal child was happy.
Your vampire child, content.

Give me back your heartbeat, mother.
Give me back your blood.

This time I'll harvest you like grain.
This time I'll pluck you like ripe fruit.

◆   ◆   ◆

Transit of Venus

All at once a woman suffocates
her lover's theories with a kiss.
Late that day, in a shaded alcove,
a boy attempts a book;
he is assaulted by honeysuckle.
Young girls' nipples grow tender
from the breeze of roses
swaying under bees.

These are the preliminaries.

The beams of houses start to breathe.
The mountains sweat attar of stone.
Soon the festivals begin, the sacrifices.

A fleshy woman sways across a vivid lawn.
The day is fiercely hot. A stone fountain
ringed with doves, a green pool into which
she gazes, the sun a halo behind her head.
She smiles, narrows her eyes,
breaks her image with a sudden hand,

and glides at last away.

♦   ♦   ♦

Maeve in Summer

Look at me:

    white mountains

    veined with gold

Listen to me:

    wind on the sea,

    wind over grass

Wander in me:

    bright meadows

    in dark forests

Breathe me:

    sweet herbs underfoot

    and roses, roses

Taste me:

    honey, salt, blood

    salt, blood, honey

Touch me:

    hold the world

    reach the stars

◆   ◆   ◆

Cybele's Song

I am a lion savaging my prey.
I am a gazelle brought to earth.

I am the beginning of desire.
I am the end of all thirst.

—weather rushes across my face—
clouds, rain, sun—oh—

I am the center of the sun.
I am the ice core of a comet.

I can never be contained.
I am vast as mountains.

—weather rushes across my face—
clouds, rain, sun—oh—

I am flower, I am stone,
I am blood and the bloodied.

I am the beginning of desire.
I am the end of all thirst.

—weather rushes across my face—
clouds, rain, sun—oh—

◆   ◆   ◆

Strength

I ask myself, how can I hold a lion
in such small hands? How dare I even touch
my palm to its huge head? An Amazon
is suited to this task, not me. Such
power ripples beneath its golden coat
I feel no match for it. Its amber eyes
look deeply into mine. I feel its throat
throb beneath my hands. We deify
such power, worship it, submit, defer,
while all the time we hate it. How dare this brute
be so beautiful? So free, so pure?
How do I dare contain such attributes?
The only way that I can play this part:
to be a woman with a lion's heart.

◆   ◆   ◆

Altar of the South

crimson silk
scarlet candles

uncut rubies
and red jade

fresh sweet cherries
a flask of claret

a lion's tooth
a cardinal's wing

an old spoked wheel
one lump of coal

a torch of pitch
one single rose

a drop of blood
in a garnet vial

♦   ♦   ♦

The Divine Sons Praise Saule As She Dances on the Hilltop

Who is the dancer in the south
who pauses on the noontime hill,

her eyes so kind, her rosebud mouth
so tender, who is she who stands

at noon there on the thin ridge
between the birth and death of day?

Who dances on the narrow bridge
of life and death? Who decks the world

with fringes from her silver shawl?
Who makes the sea into a ring

of gold? Who is that woman, all
round and full and beautiful?

Who but the darling sun,
who but the mother of light,

who but the brilliant one,
who but our sweet lover.

No one dances so brightly,
no one sparkles as she does,

no one moves more lightly,
no one brings such delight.

We praise her sleek strong thighs,
we praise her silver feet.

We praise her flashing eyes,
we praise her silver hair.

She is our darling one,
she is the mother of light,

who but the brilliant sun
dances at noon in the south.

◆   ◆   ◆

Noon

One moment of stillness.

An open field in summer, brilliant light, heat rising. The sun an eye overhead, wide open to the world.

Everything grows towards this moment. From the middle of night, light has been growing. From the heart of winter, light has been growing.

Everything is at its peak. Seeds have sprouted and grown, flowered and been fertilized. Flowering women, full of life, make life within themselves. This is the moment towards which everything yearns.

The day, all blank potential just a few hours ago, has taken shape. From numberless possibilities, I selected tasks. I moved, I danced, within the shape the day has taken. There has never been a day exactly like it, the way the light strikes the work under my hands, the way the air feels as I press towards my yearning goals.

Everything is underway. Power charges the atmosphere.

I pause and rise from my tasks. I survey the world, changed by my hands, as the sun watches from her southern station. Everything is full and rich and good.

One moment of stillness, then I begin again.

◆　　◆　　◆

The Buck at Noontime

Magic is something
you do not recognize
when it happens,

something that
ordinary.

Yes.

That is what you said,
afterwards.
Remember?

At dawn, at dusk,
across the nettles and willows,
under the sighing pines,

we would see
roe deer, fallow deer,
staring at us from the tall
dying grass—sometimes

a single doe, sometimes
two or three, once
a herd of seven
but never
before
at midday
at the crossroad
a single buck

holding us with steady gaze
until you said

If I move will he run?

You danced in front of him.
I watched him watching you.
You called and sang.

He never moved.

In the long space
between us, the long time
between us, something passed.

What passed is the stuff
of legend. I could tell
it that way. I could say:

Two children, lost in
the forest and crying
for home, were saved by
an angel of light; or,

animals called to twins
in a stone town, called
them by secret names
into a magic forest; or,

a man and woman
sought initiation into
the languages of winds
and birdsong; these are stories,

true stories
told by those
who saw something,
something ordinary

—a buck
at noontime
at the crossroad—

and knew magic,
and had no words for it

for all the stories
say the same thing,
all the stories tell us
how magic speaks:

in a voice so common,
so familiar, that we
create prayers and myths
to capture and belie its
sacred ordinariness.

Something happened to us:

We saw a buck
at noontime
at the crossroads,

we saw, at an ordinary
crossroads, the horned
god of the forest,
in blazing noon sun,

an ordinary buck
at the crossroads
of our lives,
at the day's meridian,

in the dreamtime
of the day,
an ordinary road
and an antlered deer.

Something happened to us,
in that ordinary moment:

Oh! you have broken
your perfect silence,
you have spoken
in movement and stasis,
horned god of life's changes;
you have shown us
the resurrection of death,
horned god of time's passages;

you have shown us the way,
guardian of crossroads,
angel of blue flowers,
height of the sun's blaze.

Everything we feel is true.
Every day is magic.
Everything we feel is true.

Yes.
We remember.
Yes.

◆   ◆   ◆

Fire-Feast

In the middle of the city the men
feel a sudden tenderness above the ears.
As the sun sets they lie down,
heads throbbing. As the moon rises
horns push out like seedlings
from the temples of all the men.

Most sleep through the hot night
and wake exhausted wet with sweat,
full of dreams they can't remember.
All day at work they snap warily at other
men, look weakly after all the women.
All day they search their pockets for lost keys.

Only a few rise in the moonlight,
heads full of antlers, to seek
the women dancing on the leaves.
Only a few men know the power of stags
dancing through them as they are ridden
by the eager women of the night.

And the next day, and the next,
we know these men when we meet them.
We see them from the corners of our eyes
turning into animals, turning back, turning.
We know them with our doe skin,
we know them with our steaming breath.

◆   ◆   ◆

Litany of Fire

Ash, apple, alder,
>*Bonfire, bonefire,*

Birch, beech and banyan,
>*Death pyre, needfire,*

Cherry and cedar,
>*Wildfire, balefire,*

Devilwood, dragontree,
>*Greenfire, seedfire.*

Elm, elder, ebony,
>*Bonfire, bonefire,*

Fir, fig and filbert,
>*Death pyre, needfire,*

Gingko and goldenrain,
>*Wildfire, balefire,*

Hemlock and hornbeam,
>*Greenfire, seedfire.*

Ironwood, juniper,
>*Bonfire, bonefire,*

Katsura, kentia,
>*Death pyre, needfire,*

Larch, locust, laurel,
>*Wildfire, balefire,*

Myrtle, madroña,
>*Greenfire, seedfire.*

Nutmeg and olive,
   Bonfire, bonefire,
Oak, osage orange,
   Death pyre, needfire,
Pine, poplar, pawpaw,
   Wildfire, balefire,
Quince, redbud, rowan,
   Greenfire, seedfire.

Spruce, strongbark, sumac,
   Bonfire, bonefire,
Tamarisk, tamarack,
   Death pyre, needfire,
Willow, witch-hazel,
   Wildfire, balefire,
Yew and zelkova,
   Greenfire, seedfire.

Smoke tree and smoke thorn,
   Bonfire, bonefire,
Flame of the forest,
   Death pyre, needfire,
Firewheel, firethorn,
   Wildfire, balefire,
All come to ashes,
   Greenfire, seedfire.

    ♦   ♦   ♦

Freya's Love Charm

I would have you lying on your back
in the high meadow at noon.

I would have the meadow grass
stroke your face in the shy wind.

I would have the wind, emboldened,
press open the collar of your woolen shirt.

I would have the wool grow heavy
on your chest, faintly damp and close.

I would have your damp chest need
suddenly to be cooled in the fragrant air.

I would have the cooling air press
hard against your damp dark nipples.

I would have your own slow hardness
bring back the memory of my tongue.

I would have the memory of my breasts
come back to you in a warm flood.

I would have a warm cry flood from you
as you recall the firmness of my hips.

I would have the firmness of your cry
draw me from my narrow daily path

to where I would find you, lying there,
on your back in the high meadow at noon.

♦　♦　♦

Garland Sunday, and She Calls Her Lover to Join Her on the Mountain

How many years since you pressed
that first kiss upon me, up on
the hilltop in the shining season?
I laughed and filled your mouth
with bilberries. I laughed, you
filled my mouth with love.

The next year we were joined,
we climbed the mountain
arm in arm, smiling at the
courting couples. The next year
I walked slowly, full of love;
the next year, and the next,

and now the years all run together
and now I cannot remember
which year my brother died, which
year your mother died, and always
before us the mountain, its gray
green presence a reminder of summer

and always, at this time, the climb,
always the climbing, for what is life
but seasons passing, what is love
but memories and ceremonies—
what is love but a pledge taken
on a midsummer hill and kept?

◆   ◆   ◆

Praisesong for Her

She is a tree in a circle of stones.
She is a crossroad at noon.
She is a breeze in the red mountain ash.

She is a hill on a night without stars.
She is a tear of the sun.
She is the moon on the ripening grass.

She is a hawk in the circling sky.
She is the eye of a hound.
She is a fish in the river of glass.

She is a berry of red mountain ash.
She is the seed of bright grasses.
She is a stone in the river of glass.

She is the sigh as time passes.

◆   ◆   ◆

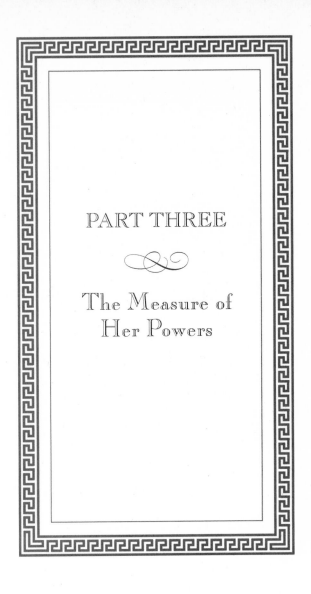

PART THREE

The Measure of
Her Powers

Fall

Now comes the time of reckoning, the season of limits.

There will never be more than there is now. Harvest is done, the cellars are full. Two seasons of growth have led to this richness, this security, this abundance. Now is the time to celebrate the plenty that work and time have wrought. Now, the time to feast with friends, share the bounty, toast the work well done.

Now is the time, as well, of endings. For nothing more is growing. Nothing more will grow this year. There will never be more than there is now. The winds of autumn descend to tear seed from stalk, to scatter what has not been captured.

This is the time to decide what will die. Not all of last spring's calves and lambs and ducklings can be fed through the winter. Some will die, and in dying provide food. It is a season of decisions. And of prophecies: For as other life dies, it foreshadows our own deaths. The taste of death is in the air in fall. On our tongues, too, the taste of death: of plants that give us their seeds, of animals that give us their flesh.

Such communion! As we pick the pumpkin from its frozen, shrivelled stalk, as we press juice from apple's flesh, as we tear out carrot life by its roots, we taste the deepest knowledge: that we need others to survive. That we breathe only because something has died. That we make our own flesh of the flesh of our world.

Never in the seasons of our life do we feel more responsible.

As she moves through autumn, a woman feels a passionate connection with all life. Yet, wise in the seasons of living, she can be unsentimental, even pitiless. She does not try to nurture everything and everyone, for she knows not all can—should—survive. She becomes selective. There is enough of everything—strength, love, passion, lust—everything but time.

Time, she knows, grows short. Nothing seems endless anymore. Her life grows full of endings: parents and friends die, animals she has loved disappear in a gasp, dreams fade beyond reclaiming. She does not recognize, when the deaths start, that fall has begun. But later, she will remember: After that one, it was never the same. Never again will she hold a living body without knowing the fragility of its life, the closeness of its death.

She finds that she has limits. Her energy falters, her mind drifts, her patience snaps. She begins to husband herself, to save herself for what really matters. She has seen enough to guess the trajectory of most events, to hold herself back from repeating old mistakes. She knows now that some energy is wasted. So sometimes she seems parsimonious, unwilling to expend in waste. But other times she is generous. That old coat? Give it away. That pretty pin? Oh, do take it. The half-finished book? No, it's yours. She does not need to cling to what she has outlasted. Things leave her: She does not need it all.

Fall consumes a woman many times before and after middle life, whenever the time demands that she become decisive. She empties her womb of a conception; she leaves a convent, a marriage, a career; she puts a loved old pet to sleep. She cleans a closet, gives away old books, cuts off her hair. Autumn moods find her free and vibrant, impatient of delusions, ready to do whatever she needs to do.

For she knows what she needs, and she wants it fiercely. For every false dream that dies, a true one is remembered. She climbs mountains to stand in alpenglow, she gallops out on a magnificent horse, she paints her secrets and nightmares. She bears a last and cherished child; she remembers passion with an old friend; she writes her own, her individual, story. She knows what memories she needs to store, to provide her winter years.

The autumn woman moves towards dreamtime. Though she knows her limits, she has also felt limitless. She has known the ineffable. She wakes at night from dreams of high windy places where small blue flowers bloom, and she knows in her bones that such places exist. Luminous beings appear in her dreams and pull her towards them. She recognizes the dust of infinity in a windstorm, the fragrance of timelessness in a fire.

There is a transcendent energy about her, but she remains rooted in life's imminent realities. In her eyes you see the fire of primal knowledge: the knowledge of life and death. She knows that she will not escape this life alive. And so she embraces it, moment by moment by moment.

♦   ♦   ♦

Hera Alone, on the Mountain

From this height I can see
everything. I watch the day
recede, I watch the light
fade into red, I watch
the brown leaves fall to earth.
It is time to strip to the bone.
Time to measure the worth
of each moment, to catch
the last ones left before night.
Soon enough red fades to gray.
Soon enough we cease to be.

Look there: An eagle rises
as the first star gleams.
Now listen: Far away
an owl's deep moaning song
cuts through the chilling air.
I am standing here alone.
Standing, head back, breasts bare
to the wind. I belong
to the earth now, the sky,
to myself and to my dreams,
with no masks left, no disguises.

You who would love me now
beware. I am all fire
and blood. I have no time
for those who cannot feel
the way through flesh to soul.

My life is now half-gone.
But each night left is whole.
Each day can now reveal
how life is most sublime
when fastened to desire.
From here, all time is now.

♦   ♦   ♦

Evening

Shadows. Shade. Pools of darkness. Streaks of light.

The way outlines dissolve. The way everything grows soft. The way this world looks when you can walk through it into another.

Deliquescence. Dissolution.

Shadows losing their edges in the slant light. No hard endings, sharp beginnings. Penumbra softening each tree and fading leaf, each rock, each drooping flower.

Everything growing watery. Things fading into each other like ink.

No limits. No borders. No boundaries.

Dreams drifting, fragmentary, beautiful.

No outlines in the world, no separations. Dead mouths speaking as white moths wing towards the dying light.

Under the sea, the richness, the blue richness.

A waterfall over quartz. Bluebirds singing.

Between. Between.

A dark bog.

Drifting.

The body. Liquid.

Flowing.

Everything. Passing. Between.

♦   ♦   ♦

The Star

One woman, many stars:
Balance in unbalance.
I hold the center,
water unto water.

One tree, one woman:
Similarity in distinction.
Water unto water:
stars beyond stars.

Mountains and plain:
Connection in difference.
Stars beyond stars,
bird on the wing.

Small stars and large:
Identity in essence.
Water unto water,
my center to the center.

Image and viewer:
Meaning in randomness.
My center, your center:
water unto water.

♦ ♦ ♦

Litany of Water

Hammerhead, bonnethead, yellow and blue.
Tiger and cat and angel and sand.
Basking shark, angle shark, whale shark too.
Tiger and cat and angel and sand.

Stingaree, starry skate, manta, electric ray.
Devil, torpedo, giant butterfly.
Guitarfish, chimera, spotted eagle, hey.
Devil, torpedo, giant butterfly.

Porgy and bony gar, catfish and sucker.
Golden shiner, silverfin, chained moray.
Worm eel and snake eel and blotched eel and others.
Golden shiner, silverfin, chained moray.

Oscellated moray, alewife and tarpon.
Herring and sardine, anchovy, shad.
Brook trout and smelt and humpbacked salmon.
Herring and sardine, anchovy, shad.

Four-winged flying fish, pearl side and seahorse.
Trumpet and cornet and pipe and key.
Barracuda, sand-diver, sand lance of course.
Trumpet and cornet and pipe and key.

Goatfish and sailfish and frigate and mackerel.
Stripe and blue marlin, tunny and chub.
Pompano, amber-jack, look-down and angel.
Stripe and blue marlin, tunny and chub.

Perch and grouper, phoebe and surgeon.
Man-of-war, dolphin, crappie and bass.
Snapper and porgy, croaker and sturgeon.
Man-of-war, dolphin, crappie and bass.

Sea raven, sea robin, star-gazer, fluke.
Dragonet, wry-mouth and naked sole.
Unicorn filefish, flounder and geoduck.
Dragonet, wry-mouth and naked sole.

◆   ◆   ◆

Edain's Charm for Lasting Love

Join me one gold day by an autumn lake.
Walk there beside me, hand in hand.
Reach down to pick a golden leaf.
            Never leave. Never leave.

Join me on a leafy hillside facing
west to the darkening sea. Turn your face
towards me as the tide sweeps out
            and returns. And returns.

Join me in a turning circle dance
in a field of sunset-ripened grain.
Hold me as I age to gold.
            Join me there. Join me there.

◆   ◆   ◆

Pomona Sings to the Old Woman

You stood there,
a splendid autumn tree,

your trunk so firm
and strong, your hair

a radiance of flame,
your limbs brushed red,

and all I could think
was how strong the sap

pulsed in you, strong
as spring, all I could

think was how deep
you went, all that

rich sap in you,
deeper and deeper and

deeper and how I wanted
to pull your limbs down

to me then, there, under
the open sky, and how

I wanted you then,
there, to flame up

at my touch, how
I wanted to fall

burning, burning, burning,
and ignite all the hills

in a ring of bright flame
around you, old tree,

old splendid woman,
old treasure, old heart.

How I wanted you then.
How I'm wanting you now.

◆　◆　◆

The Goddess Instruction Manual, Part Three: How to Make Love like Oshun

1. Begin with fingertips.
Read every burning tree,
red fruit, blue stone.
Move on to wind and water.
Then seasons, futures.

2. When adept, try this:
Read the body. First your own.
Its history and poetry,
its intimate geographies.
Keep eyes closed.
See with touch.
Memorize yourself.

3. Touch each other.

4. Continue as above.

5. Continue as above.

6. The world, the eyes
open. O wonder!
O newness!
O fragrant air!
O blue sound!
O body radiant
with imperfection!

7. Everything should be
liquid at this point.
Liquid and golden.
Dive and plunge.
Swim. Frolic.

8. Something
shattering:
crystal,
purple glass,
dark blue porcelain.
Break apart.

9. Dissolve in light.
Dissolve into pale stars.

10. Keep looking.
Keep touching.

11. The word is:
yes.
The world is:
yes.

12. Continue as above.

◆　◆　◆

Lover

Come. She is waiting.

She waits where she always waits, there behind the veil.

In one hand, she holds a mirror. She does not look into its glassy face. She knows she is not beautiful, that she does not need to be beautiful, she knows that she is beauty itself, beauty that does not need a mirror to know itself.

She does not need a mirror to know herself. The mirror is for you, to know yourself.

She is always waiting, there behind the veil. Come.

She is lifting her hair up, away from her shoulders, piling it atop her head, letting small tendrils escape to touch her face. She moves her shoulders slightly, as though a heavy weight had been released. She bows her head and looks at you.

Her hair is the veil. She is waiting behind it. Come.

She puts her hand on your skin. It feels smooth and strong. You cover her hand with yours, which feels smooth and strong.

She moves her hand. She is strong and sure. You move your hands. You grow strong and sure. She is dancing under your hands. No: She is the dance and the dancer and the danced. And you are the dance, the dancer, the danced.

You part her veils, one and then another, one and then another. There is no end to the beauty you find in her, no end to what she finds in you. She is beauty. You become beauty. You, she, the world, the light, beauty.

Light glows from her eyes, golden, as she looks at you. Light glows from your eyes, golden, as you look at her.

You glow together, golden. Light veils you.

Come. She is waiting. Come.

◆　◆　◆

Maeve's Discourse on Beauty

Many things are beautiful,
but one thing is most beautiful:

there, against the dark pool,
his body white as a trout,

his hair so dark and soft,
his face so sweetly shaped,

broad above, narrow below,
his body firm and spotless,

broad above, narrow below,
ah, and the branch he carries:

mountain ash, berries red
as his own sweet lips, a wand

firm and lovely as his own—
nothing is more beautiful

than my love, swimming to me
across a dark pool, while I lie

waiting for him in the shade
of the one tree on my island.

◆   ◆   ◆

Waning Moon

Almost the young moon, this sliver, this shining crescent. Same shape reversed. Same pattern cut from cloth of night. Same dance danced with winds of night.

The moon's boat turns towards the dark port as tide ebbs towards the heart of earth.

I stand in soft darkness, ready to embrace the great change. No more will I say this is the moon's decline, that it fades and dies, that its power wanes. No: This is a different birth, a surging into change, into the unknown within the known.

I open my arms to the sky and breathe in the night.

Into the dark moistness of my body, I receive the darkness.

The boundary between inner and outer dissolves. Growing darkness outside, unknown familiar within. The edges of my body soften the edges of my mind.

Somewhere a waterbird calls, once, sharply, a wild laugh. I ride a cascade of loss and joy and fear and yearning, all of them at once, all equally fervent and surrounding. Everything is change, everything in flux. I am in flux. I descend into deeper darknesses, holding my arms above me as I turn slowly, breathing heavily in the dark.

Breathing in the dark.

Above, the moon glides down to set on black lake waters. Again, the bird calls out, its laughter a great swoop upwards, then a plummet down.

Breathing in the dark.

♦　♦　♦

Venus of Laussel

You rise in my dreams
like the power of stone,
breaking the glass door
between wind and the body.
You are the measurer:

blood of my moons,
lines of my years.
A thread of breath
connects me to time,
wind in my blood,
a thread to your womb.
Thirteen short lines—

You rise, then are gone.

◆   ◆   ◆

Altar of the West

a cobalt bowl
brimming with water

a necklace of sequins
or mermaid scales

a velvet pouch
heavy with coins

a black mirror
framed with shell

amber perfumed oil
redolent of spices

a brass trident
a golden salter

two silver chalices
a crystal vial of tears

◆   ◆   ◆

Harvesting

Raw wind chafes my face, stings my reddening cheeks. Earth warms roots while air brittles yellowing leaves. Light diminishes. I gather and gather and gather.

Can I name a single time as harvest? Spring brings seedling lettuce, early chives, wild morels. Early summer, luxuriance of strawberries, authority of sorrel, the green snap of peas. High summer, and the trickle swells to a torrent that cascades as fall approaches and everything ripens all at once. Flying seeds cloud the air. The roadsides are lush with seedheads. Everywhere promises, promises.

I fall behind. Inevitably. Beans split open to seed themselves. In leafy shadow, squashes swell huge and green. Even crows and raccoons cannot steal all the tomatoes. In the crowded garden, I gather and gather.

In a delirium of plenty, boundaries disappear. Richness, richness: velvet colors, taste of smoke, sounds soft as alderblow. Effortless work. The seasons of the heart. Death everywhere, feeding life. Life everywhere.

I stand for a moment, head bent back, listening to the last call of geese as they skein southwards. Near me, a squirrel falls silent. Then I lift my rake, the squirrel chatters, and gathering begins again.

Abundance and choice. Abundance is choice. The cellar is full. Life is full. There is no need for more.

Then a row of overlooked peppers calls out. A stand of rose hips. A last flush of strawberries, tiny, deeply sweet.

When that white day comes when all seems done, carrots still crispen secretly under straw, onions sharpen, sage gleams silver.

Harvest is over.

Harvest is never over.

♦ ♦ ♦

Caer's Song to Her Beloved

Who sings to you?
>   The sea ends. The sky begins.
>   Swans flew towards me in a dream.

Where is yesterday?
>   Ancient gold from the sea.
>   Songs of the past, in the wind.

Why this opening?
>   The harvest is complete.
>   Stars wheel over the stones.

When will I come to you?
>   The sun sets. The moon rises.
>   Dim fire blazes into life.

♦   ♦   ♦

Mabon

She has been running for so long.

She does not remember when she began. She has always been running, running, hurtling forward, headlong, passion in her heart and limbs, not thinking of the goal, only running, running.

She is hot and wet. She is wet with heat.

Her breath comes in deep gasps. Her searing heart expands.

Everything blurs.

Everything.

Running.

And then.

She stops in her tracks. She stares. A strong woman, panting, stares back at her. Eyes blazing with force and heat. A mirror? A mirage? A perfect twin? Hair tangled with sweat. Her? Another? Who?

And then.

Running, everything blurring.

Searing heart. Breath in deep gasps.

Hot and wet. Wet with heat.

Running, hurtling headlong forward, passion in heart and limbs, no goal, only running, running. Running.

Running.

◆   ◆   ◆

Housemagic

You descend the stairs at midnight.
You walk through the sleeping house.
Light surrounds you in the silent dark.

Was it a nightmare woke you?

You pour a glass of water.
You sit by the window, beside that
cobalt vase filled with blue flowers.
Into the dark blue center of sleep
you slip again, into the blue
blackness of true forms, into
the fragmented pool of meaning.

There, on the boundary of
boundlessness, you dream
and, dreaming, remember what
you have not utterly forgotten:
how your kitchen always has at least one
witch's broomstick, how clove and garlic
are domesticated on your spicerack,
how everything has power.

But you remember only how, not
why. And so your power finds
its limits: You can raise
the bread but you cannot
tame the nightmares that
pasture in the silent house.
You have forgotten the way
to the wildness within you,
to the instinct for order.

Now as you sleep you dream
of a half-remembered house: bedraggled
as old lace, its stairs rot into wooden
filigrees, its attic suffocates in private
dust. And in its flooded basement
the rivers, the sewers of the world
breed terrifying marvels. Because
the house grows wild, disorderly, all
the gardens in the world turn treacherous
and forests strangle on themselves.

But in this house all change is possible.
Some corners—left or right, dining room
or pantry—grow shiny with significance.
A ladder leans against a wall.
Sheer white curtains billow.
A floor creaks. A door closes.

When you wake in the blue hour
before dawn, you remember
an old house with stairways that
lead to attics that connect to trees.
You remember all the paths.

And remembering, you know how
to make the necessary changes
to pull the day towards night, to
let all things revel in meaning,
dreaming the world's secrets like
the favored habitat of blueberries,
like the seasoning of rosehips,
like the uses of lichen and moss.

On a bureau you collect
a chipped mirror with a
woman's face, a stem of bedstraw that died aslant, your
sister's candlesticks,

an old pot with a mother's
belly, a box covered with
dusty embroideries.

Then, in another room:
rocks in a spiral pattern,
a branch that sang in a
mysterious and certain way,
a whitened bone.
A gray owl feather,
a small pile of seeds.
All in a certain order.

Now, when you sleep
you build a round tower,
you cut new windows,
you carve a pool in shade.
A candle burns beside you
as you dream. It flickers
sometimes in the cool breeze.
Outside your window, a single
leaf breaks against stone
as it falls from the gnarled oak.

And you dream of being in the power
of grasses, frail patched lace,
filigree seedheads, mist of renewal,
reckless with shedding. You dream
your hair full of seeds, your hair
a cushion for seeds to rest on,
you dream you were born to move
seeds to new lands, you dream
purposes and reasons, you are
full of thoughtless utility.

And sleeping there, you feel
your dream and the world's
dream join. A path stretches
out before you, the path from
childhood: at its end, a new
tree is taking root, its taproot
drinking your heart's blood.

And, when you wake and move
through the dim silent room,
you know that the wind of your
daily dance brings a storm to
an old forest on another continent,
and that the fall of its giants
leaves room for new growth.

Midnight: You open the door.
A horse comes galloping.
There are no horses where
you live. But she is there,
wearing no saddle, no reins.

With blueblack eye she invites
you. She kneels as you mount.

This is where the dream would
end, if this were a dream.
But it is not, and so
the next thing
you feel is
the rush of wind
in your hair.

♦   ♦   ♦

Climax

We say this happened, then this, and then this.

We never say: This did not happen, here is where we did not turn, that is not the one, things were different.

To tell one story is to select one strand of a fine fabric and pull it. Alone, it has a length and width and texture. But in that great cloak from which it came, that strand formed unimaginable patterns.

So many stories. Each moment opening out to endlessness. Each moment innumerable stories intersecting, each worthy of telling. Some playing out on the surface, others shadowing what we know. But there are more, even more, wild rich rumorings, lavish weaves of possibility.

When, from all possibilities, we choose one strand: At that moment, we enter time. At that moment, we believe we know where the story yearns and why. At that moment, everything changes.

That single thread of story. A rope, a noose. Lace, tweed. The material of fable. The goods of a life.

♦   ♦   ♦

Amulets and Talismans

There is no safety in the wood
without one. There is no rest,
alone in the dark house, without
some charm

against soft forms rising
from salty depths, against
unknown sounds, untrackable
odors, the sudden taste of metal—

the old book from another
state, the broken mended glass,
those antique instruments
of rhythm and of wind, even that

ring with the uncut blue stone
you twist to dissipate
the thunders of the ordinary,
these are magic
against what dances wild and
groaning in the fairy

circle of your skull.

◆　◆　◆

The Witch Threatened

someone keeps tying knots in all
my nets and opening mouths
of scissors and uncorking
essences and herbs and that

someone today tricked me out
of a curse, tripping
right into my hammock
when even my apron was off

and I lay there fluting
against the spruce arms of
my lover—he would be
dead this instant if I knew

his name to spell
backwards or his turned-
away face to form and
melt against my warm

palm, my red hand
closing on his secrets
while invisible songs
singe and glow as he goes

◆   ◆   ◆

The Witch Complains of Hansel

There he squats, day after day,
crouched in my bedroom like a rat,
gnawing scraps of air, snapping
at my ankles as I pass.

I fan breadsticks before his face
to tempt his appetite but he
writhes away ungratefully. When
I bring soup his dwarfish feet
make swimming, struggling signs.
Nothing interests him, not fresh
mushrooms folded into omelets,
not my soft spiced gingerbread.

At night I hear the rasping breath
from the righthand corner near the closet.
He is gulping up air. It is filling him up
like a blimp. His little rat eyes
glow like a terrified nightlight.

I lie there fretting, night after night.
If only he would eat. I have tried
everything. I've offered all I have
to give. I am losing patience. Tomorrow
I will turn him into a greenbean.
I will snap him in two.

◆ ◆ ◆

She Hexes Newscasters

What else could I do? For weeks
it had been one intolerable
word after another, war and
war and war again and it seemed

so easy. A word from me, and
songs sprayed from their mouths,
automatic carols: praise
for the caliber of clouds
and the blue shrapnel sky,
the bombardment of rain,
praise for the maneuvers
of finches and ravens, praise—

but it is not enough, even though
it is my strongest spell, making
beauty out of words. I repeat it,
I repeat it nightly, I burn
blue candles just to keep them
singing. Oh I want real power:

that soldiers, aiming at men's
hearts, see into them and stop,
that presidents invoke old
powers—earth and wind and
all their deputies—that
generals sit before their maps
telling rapt stories of the dawn.

♦   ♦   ♦

She Visits the Trollwife

This hill stinks.
Cranberries rot soft,
a dead flesh warning.

She waves her seven-
fingered hand to open
the spruce door,
climbs the wings
of children to her cone
house, her cauldron
red in the glass dawn.

Some things are beyond
my power. She who could
spell me to death
considers my challenge,
rubs dust of chaparral
into her slow skin.

A white horse
drifts in the window,
shrinks into smoke,
before she replies.

    ◆   ◆   ◆

The Measure of Her Powers

Deep in her favorite
forest, on the best
path home, she—

proud of her skills, tapping
reverently the humming birch,
remembering to step aside

from the night path of
the owl, she the diviner,
proud of her skill—forgot

that every forest is magical,
all paths are sometimes
the wrong way—she got

lost, ambushed by dwarf spruce,
trapped by dogwood that led
on—each leaf pointing to the next

impasse—alders raking her
face, willow thickets repaying
her neglect of their winter

needs—the occasional lack of
necessary homage, careless nights
when neither green nor soft gray

reminded her—she
spiralled, straying farther,
further—were there

ravens here, were there
wolves, were there
bears—

◆　◆　◆

Night of the Black Mirror

Hold up the crystal.
See who will die this winter.
Catch the floating apple.
See who will die this winter.
Cut the honeyed cake.
See who will die this winter.

This is the night of games.

This is the night when the curtain
lifts briefly in the wind of stars.
This is the night when the veil
shreds in the wind's shards.
This is the night when we gaze
into the face of the black mirror.

This is the night of prophecies.

The black mirror is a glass
veil over a deep well.
The black mirror is a glass
eye from an old skull.
The black mirror is a glass
jewel in the ring of time.

This is the night the glass breaks.

◆   ◆   ◆

A Vision of Hunger in Flesh

The owl flies low tonight. The hare leaps high.
There are nights when life ordains a chase,
nights like this, when nothing fears to die.

There is no sound, no bird or rabbit cry
to mark the moment they begin the race.
The owl flies low tonight. The hare leaps high.

Across the snowy fields like man and bride
they dance towards their intentional embrace.
There are nights when nothing fears to die.

And as the owl descends in one slow glide,
we lay on hands like priests dispensing grace.
The owl flies low tonight. The hare leaps high.

Watching from the house, we're sanctified
by need. Communion shows its primal face
on nights like this, when nothing fears to die.

The dance of life and death makes us allies
as hunger raises us beyond disgrace.
The owl flew low tonight. The hare knew why.
There are nights when nothing fears to die.

♦   ♦   ♦

In His Last Moments, Oisin
Praises Niamh of the Golden Hair

What was it worth, my time with you?
Easy to say:
Amber is more common.
Gold worthless in comparison.
Spring dawn far less beautiful.

What drew me to your side?
Easy to say:
Your waterfall laughter.
Your breath, caught in surprise.
Light sheening off your hair.

Why did we ever part?
Easy to say:
The wheel, the ceaseless wheel.
Perfection's sheer monotony.
The memory of death.

What use is this body now?
Easy to say:
None, unless to pleasure you.
None, without you near.
None, except to make you smile.

What would I give to be with you?
Easy to say:
Every earthly comfort.
Moments of faint joy.
The chance at rebirth.

♦   ♦   ♦

The Old Song of the Tribes

The sky draws its curtain
across the season. Any day
now it will snow, curtaining

the footprints in the soft earth
we made today, but any day in this life
or another, if I meet you, the earth's

pull will be upon us, the mark of the forest
will be on us, indelible handprints, birthmarks.
We will know each other in city or forest,

despite continents and oceans, we will know
each other as much, as little as
we know ourselves, as much as we know

what the mind is, what the body can be. Amidst
all the changing, our souls will remain
true to each other. The rest can be mist.

♦   ♦   ♦

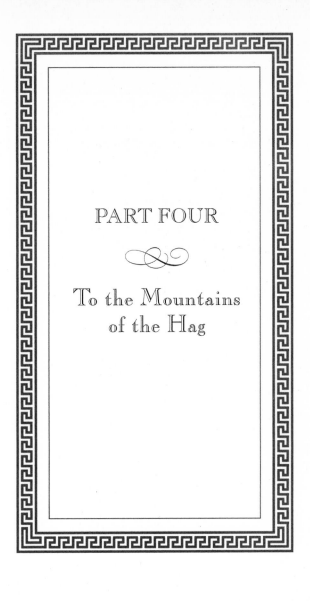

PART FOUR

To the Mountains
of the Hag

Winter

Finally comes the time of withdrawal, the hidden time.

It is as though the world sleeps under a gray cloak. Everything is still and silent. It is though the world sleeps under a gray veil.

Look to the massive tree whose branches lift towards pearly skies. It fingers the low clouds. Its branches break and fall in the heavy winds. They droop and break in the heavy snows. Cut them: no sap runs. The tree seems empty, dead.

Look for the bear and its friends: you will not find them. Earth hides the sleeping bear, the hibernating frog, the coiled immobile snake. Stillness settles over the forests of the north as birds skein away, taking song southwards. Rabbit fur drifts into whiteness. Grouse feathers drift into whiteness.

Life has moved to the center, to its hidden darknesses. Bulbs rest, roots sleep, trees go dormant. Stillness settles over the world.

Yes, this is darkness before dawn. Yes, it is rest before new growth. But who—watching a few brown birds light in empty branches and pull at wizened berries—who can believe how close life lies to the wintry surface?

Yet it is there. A warm spell brings out pussywillows. Tiny crocuses and hyacinth brave the snow to bloom, color against winter's gray. Witch-hazel bursts into frayed blossoms. Life rests; it has not ended.

Winter's woman too is gray, but floods color at a moment's warmth.

Winter's woman is a still pond, mirroring the world from her calm eyes. Winter's woman is rooted, coiled, full of potential.

There is wisdom in winter. Each season has its own wisdom, but winter's includes all. What is invisible in growing times becomes plain in the dry cold of winter. From winter, one can remember spring, summer, fall, can see all their patterns. This is the time when all seems clear.

And all seems complete. There is not yet a call to begin again, for beginnings will come soon enough. This is the fallow time. This is the time of rest.

This is also the time of visions. For as the world sleeps, as the woman's energies withdraw into a coiled serpent at the base of her spine, the inner eye widens. There is so much to see beyond the world of appearances! Wisdom bestows its miraculous kaleidoscope. Spirits call from beyond time. What had been a glass wall between mind and world dissolves into a shimmering veil that blows open—often, then more often— to reveal new powers.

There is magic in all seasons, but winter's magic is most concise, most dense, most crystalline. It is diamond magic, cool and brilliant, not the fiery magic of coal. It is laser fineness, precise direction.

When winter comes to a woman's soul, she withdraws into her inner self, her deepest spaces. She refuses all connection, refutes all arguments that she should engage in the world. She may say she is resting, but she is more than resting: She is creating a new universe within herself, examining and breaking old patterns, destroying what should not be revived, feeding in secret what needs to thrive.

Winter women are those who bring into the next cycle what should be saved. They are the deep conservators of knowledge and of power. Not for nothing did ancient peoples honor the grandmother. In her calm deliberateness, she winters over truth, she freezes out falseheartedness.

Look into her eyes, this winter woman. In their gray spaciousness you can see the future. Look out of your own winter eyes. You too can see the future.

◆　◆　◆

Hera Celebrates Her Solitude

I am going down to the dark
dark places I know best.

I am going down to swim
in the warm-misted sea.

I am a hooded woman
pulling back my gray veils.

I am a cloaked woman
stepping free of my robes.

There is a mountain that
rises above the wine sea.

I will find that mountain
and sweep the clouds from her.

I will climb that mountain.
I will shine like a moon,

a dark sun,
a red star—

I will circle and
climb, circle and

climb, circle
and climb

the dark hill,
the dark hill,

to the opening,
the high windy space

where the sky
dances in waves

of red pulsing light
where the sky chimes

and the whole earth sings
like an opening flower—

◆   ◆   ◆

Yule

At last, a moment of rest.

She coils into herself like a great snake. Her long gray hair falls down over her great body, great looping spirals over breasts that rise like rounded hills, over shoulders that jut out like mountain ridges. Her great long hair covers her like a silver waterfall.

Deep stillness covers her like night.

Dark silence wraps itself into her.

Stillness, silence, coil into her, twining together with her slow breath. She could be dead, save for her slow muffled sighs, the infinitesimal lift of her vast breast, the minute flaring of her nostrils.

Behind heavy lids, her eyes move slightly. In her dream, chariots descend from remotest stars and burst up through volcanic rock, women ride behind great black horses across a pale gray sky, everything explodes with amber light. There is no rest in her dream, but its ceaseless motion rocks her into comfort and content until the difference between rest and movement becomes invisible as a dark moon in a winter sky.

In her dream of ceaseless motion, she stirs. Her great strong body shifts. Her coiling silver hair falls in great long braids to the ground.

She opens, just barely, one eye.

A shaft of sunlight. Time's amber jewel.

The sound of glass breaking into silver shards.

And she begins slowly, so slowly, to uncoil herself again.

◆   ◆   ◆

Angerona, Signaling Silence

Not that I am mute
or closed against you, not
that I have nothing to sing, nor
that pain or poverty or grief
has silenced me: no

no—

my silence is a pause
in music, a dark moon,
the moment before bleeding.
My silence is the space
between two heartbeats,
the moment of breath's fullness.

I am the woman of secrets.
I keep everything contained.

I am a mountain in long light,
a dreamer sleeping, a whale
sounding, an open eye,
watching, watching, watching.

♦   ♦   ♦

Ishtar, Ishtar

I am speaking to you
from that place beyond
words:

it is not silent for
sound starts here
its dark dancing

it is not secret for
all here is known,
familiar as the salt
taste of the body

do not say my name:
it would drive this
wordless place

away

wilderness
before
settlement

retreating

♦   ♦   ♦

Dark Moon

She is invisible.

Yes, she rises, yes she sails the sky, yes she sets. And yes, she pulls oceans in her wake, and yes she pulls the tides within us so that some secret self awakens under her dark spell and silently sings.

But invisibly.

In sunset's conflagration she hovers like a ghostly lover. In dawn's red gold she hides like memory. In a bright day she is there, shadowing the light. She is there, she is always there, even when the empty night rings with her absence as she floats veiled in light on the shadowless side of Earth.

It is midnight. I want to call on her, to open my empty heart so that, in a great flood of life, I will be filled. I raise my arms, lift them, throw back my head and stare up to the black center of the night. The sky flickers distantly. No cool and steady light, no crystal arch, no pearl eye, nothing.

And yet. And yet.

My blood a tidepool. My heart an ocean. My soul pulled to her, dark mother, dark matter, presence in absence, great mystery. Some part of me, riding always with her, invisible even to myself, deep taproot in earth, not distant or absent at all.

Invisible. Yes. Secret fullness. Yes.

Power. Yes. Yes. Yes.

I see her. Finally.

Within.

◆   ◆   ◆

Journey to the Mountains of the Hag

We are crossing the mountains
of the hooded woman,
following the trail of her cloak.

Somewhere in the hills
is a shining lake, somewhere
on the lake is a woman.

The sun rises earlier each day,
but it grows colder, colder.
What is the season of my heart?

Darkness swells about us and
sea mist surges into fog,
blinding us, blinding us.

We are following an old map,
an old story. We are following
the names on the land.

The lake we seek has no
islands in it, no cities
beneath its gray waves.

The lake is a single gray
eye, staring at the future.
The lake is a cave in time.

And the woman: swathed
in dark veils, she will be
floating on silver water.

It was dark when you
met me. It will be dark
when we meet her.

But now, for a moment, light
gleams on the gray mountains
and on the sea's pearl mist.

For an instant we see the silver
light dying on the lake's face.
At that instant, we stop.

(You ask how we navigate?
It is easy to say:

First there is heaviness
in the chest, a heartache,

restlessness, anxiety.
When you move it eases.

When you move in one direction
it eases most. Even in the cold

cutting wind, even in the gale,
moving is better than not moving.

You, too, can find her this way.
You, too, in the awful mountains,

near the dead cliffs,
near the rock barrens,

you too can find your way.
You can find your way.

Even when you are not looking
you are looking for her.)

That is how we travel, looking
but not looking. That is how we
move, knowing and not knowing.

When silver gleams upon
the lake's face, we climb
the high crag over the water.

We stop to watch and wait.
A skein of geese flies crackling
overhead, aimed like an arrow.

This is the time you find
to tell me a story: how an old
woman flew about the country

on a gray horse, how she sang
harshly at midnight and brought
the stars to earth, how she hallowed

the woods by perfect naming,
how she healed by a glance, how she
cursed by a word, how she blazed

through the world like a comet,
like a dark sun, like a dark moon,
like the dancing polar lights.

You can almost remember her
name. You can almost remember
how you were warned as a child

of this woman, what you must
say to her, what you must never
say. You can almost remember.

(How did we know when to
start, to stop? It is easy to say:

Watch for the moment when
the world tilts. There are spaces

you cannot see straight on
that open in those moments.

That is the moment to begin.
Begin in a circle and spiral inwards.

Keep on until you hear the sound
that is no sound, a sound like bees

on the moon or a horse
nickering in a dream. Watch

then the way one place rights
itself in the tilting world.)

I cannot say how many hours
pass. Cold grows around us
like moss, darkness like ivy.

But she is not here. She is not
here like an islet on the lake.
She has hidden herself from us.

In silence we descend the crag.
In silence we leave the lake.
In silence we circle home.

There was a woman in another
town, you say, who flowed like
poetry through the days and

gave her name to the land.
There was a woman in another
land, you say, who sang

wild creatures from the woods
and trees down from the hills.
Where have they gone? Where

have the women gone? Why
are we in darkness again,
swept by the chill sea winds?

(O searchers in darkness,
remember this moment. Remember

what emptiness is, remember
how cold it feels. The moment

before a journey ends is
the longest of all moments.

It is only when you abandon
the search that she can be found.)

You leave me at a crossroads near a bridge.
It is deep dark. I am alone and cold.
I have come across a world to find her
on a gleaming lake. And I have failed.

I walk down the empty street alone.
Alone, I find the key to open a door
onto a long stairway. I climb and climb
in the cold night. I climb to the top.

She is waiting, veiled, when I arrive.
I cannot see her in the gray dark.
I cannot feel her wrap herself around me
but when I wake I am coiled in her hair.

However I move, I cannot see her.
It is as though I am blind in one eye.
However I shift, something of her disappears.
However I stare, something of her hides.

Then, in a flood of trumpet light I see
the universe of her boulder face,
the length of her snaky legs,
the gray depth of her blinded eye.

(Why is she never what we imagine,
she who waits at the end of all journeys?

Easy to say: our purpose is the journey,
hers is a purpose beyond all intent.)

At the top of long stairs near an old bridge,
she holds me like a mother, like a lover.

She pierces me with her glance. She sings
stars to me. She calls my perfect name.

She surrounds me like mountains.
She floats on me, dark and silver.

She grows into me like trees, like moss.
She becomes the season of my heart.

I am a sunny lake, I am a cold sea mist.
I am darkness upon the wings of geese.

I breathe in the knowledge of my death.
And I remember all her names at once.

♦   ♦   ♦

Crone

In the center of every forest is a well of sweet water. By the time you reach it, you will be desperate with thirst. You will have been walking through the day and into the night, and the woods will have been growing darker around you, and you will have seen no water at all.

And then, a clearing lit by silver light.

You do not see her standing in the shadows. You cup your shaking hands and dip into the well. But a bony hand grasps yours.

Shaken with surprise, you look up.

She is veiled. From beneath the veil she speaks. Her voice is full of the mystery of endings. She asks what you want.

Water, you begin to say.

Then your heart is flooded with memory and need. You remember losses and pain, driven days when you burned with yearning, bleak hopelessness of abandoned dreams. Your parched throat will not let you speak. And there is not time enough to answer, for what you desire has become immeasurably and inexpressibly vast.

She is waiting.

You stand wordless before her.

She opens her arms to you, and suddenly she is all that you desire: arms to hold you, a breast to weep upon, a murmuring voice to sing in your ear, a softness that is more comfort than you have ever known.

She is sweet water in the dark forest. She is abandoned dreams restored. She is all the world at once, and all the time you need.

♦   ♦   ♦

The World

It is everything,
and the end
of everything.

The circle,
and the square
beyond the circle.

The fullness,
and the emptiness that
comes after fullness.

The four parts,
and the center
of those parts.

This is for you:
all you need,
all you want

is there for you
in this round world,
awaiting you.

◆   ◆   ◆

The End

In truth: it is a lie.

Because we live in time, we invented story. Story that gives form to the immeasurable. That fences the formless. Story that straightens the roughness of life, smooths its twists. Story that starts from here, stops somewhere, ends there.

Story that makes life a journey.

We say we made a wrong turning. We say we were just passing through. That our minds wander. That the way was straight or smooth.

But life is not the story of a journey. It is not any story at all. Nothing so simple as that. Nothing so simple as beginnings and endings.

Endings: everywhere, and constant. A word ends, a sentence, a paragraph, a poem. Small endings? All endings are small. A cell in the heart. A sharp word. An atom.

Constant too, and everywhere: beginnings. Entwined with endings, our lacy world, knotted with growth.

When is a journey over?

I disembark into adventure. What has ended? What begun?

What is the difference?

♦　♦　♦

Omens

A woman, fearing death,
hears sirens in the night,
sees dolphins leap in
candle flames, and cries

why

are they called sirens,
are they not a warning,
can there be seduction
in this danger, how can
death be beautiful?

(A wheel, far from any road,
a slug on its rim, a snail
on its axis. A raven that
flies into a woman's face,
screaming. Three footfalls
in a darkened wood.

The moment before, fear,
then abandonment of fear,
then hope, and then
abandonment of hope,

and then
the shadow of the future.)

We stare into the flame,
the fearful one and I, dimly
aware of deep movement,
dimly aware of what
rises towards us,
watching for it,

the whale that now
draws near, the future
barnacled across its back,
the one rising towards us,

the whale
that now
draws
near—

♦   ♦   ♦

The Goddess Instruction Manual,
Part Four: How to Dance with Kali

1. Recognize:

You are flame.

Blue and hot.

You do not control

your burning.

2. Calculate:

The exact surface

area of the first

tree you see today.

Include all winter buds,

abandoned nests, lost leaves.

You have just one moment.

3. Consider:

Your hand, touching your face.

A skeleton, touching a skull.

4. Practice:

Open one hand.

One finger at a time.

Small one. Ring finger.

Middle finger. Index.

Thumb. One at a time.

Then the other hand.

One finger at a time.

Now hold them out.

Wide open. Open.

5. Measure:
The depth of your heart.
The height of your dream.
The breath of your vision.
Provide examples.

6. Recognize:
You
are
flame.

7. Move:
Into
the
light.

♦   ♦   ♦

Sheila-na-Gig

You have forgotten me again.
Curious girl, you found me
once: I was the old one
sleeping in that twisted yew
and breaking rocks with angry
roots, the one you woke from
a trance as long as forests.

You pressed my knotty eyes
open to stare at me, then
stirred me open to you like
a woman waking out of
nightmares of dead children.
Then you forgot again.

As for me
I still stir like a somber
spoon in a salty stew;
I am in your blood
testing you, tasting you,
waiting for the moment
when you are done.

◆   ◆   ◆

Death Cammas

Wake in the wet dawn from dreams
of treachery. Ignore the moon
phase: This is the only day
the lily bears its blossoms.
Wear silk gloves to dig the root.
Leave one to seed the rocky soil.

Store the bulb with henbane,
belladonna, all the ancient
poisons hidden once beneath
amethyst and silver. Let it
gleam like threats. Let it
cool to dust like afternoons.

That night walk the spiral garden.
Breathe aconite and artemisia, and
picture faces rapturous in the grip
of their beauty. Pain is the entrance
to forgetfulness. Would you remember
everything, all excellence, all sorrow?

◆　　◆　　◆

Snow White on the Apple

I held it up, solid in my hands,
flesh of the tree, dense as rock,
gleaming like crimson secrets.

It smelled like earth spice.
It smelled like dusky water.
It smelled like the ghost of roses.

Of course I knew it was the apple
of forgetfulness. But oh, sister,
how much I needed to forget:

the assaults, the betrayals,
the abandonments. I did not bite
into that fruit in ignorance.

This is exactly what I wanted:
stillness, glassy beauty, peace.
This is exactly what I wanted.

♦　♦　♦

Lying Fallow

After storms, I walk the winter garden.

In bone-time, I see the world's structure: the oak's drama, the ash's dance, the curtain of alder. The shapes of innerness, the way light falls on open boughs, what it reveals of the past, the future.

A flicker of red: cardinal, that rough imperial presence.

I walk the woodland path. Without distraction of hope, I see what is ending, ready to die. The ironwood, bark twisted around its narrow frame, its roots loosening in the earth. The tilting willow, about to relax into death. The great old maple that soon will fall. Then my throat will tighten, my eyes flood. Now I look without bitterness at the past, the future.

No regrets. Only seeds. Everywhere, seeds. The past, the future. At the road, burdock holds up pointy fists. Beneath, yarrow stands, erect small soldiers. Grass catches wind, swooning to the ground and springing back. Rose hips gleam, and the last red firethorn.

The special beauty of waiting. Patience and reserve. Proud bearing, infinite vulnerability. Things seen for what they are.

Dark shadow on the snow; above me, crow calls.

♦   ♦   ♦

Altar of the North

wing feather of snowy owl
a globe of crystal quartz

ivory figure of arctic fox
yards of sheer white silk

and pieces of black fur
and dark blue candles

something simple and metal,
like nails or a knife

a faceted onyx sphere
black earthenware bowl

a round skin drum
a curl of dark hair

◆   ◆   ◆

Seeing Through the Flesh Eye

There is a race that starts when
ice locks the rivers and the sun
rises low. You are animal

in that place beneath high empty
trees that arch into the midnight sky.
You race to the needle's eye of a mountain,

the moon rising there, the star setting.
Ahead the others draw close and rush
into the narrow pass. At the moment

between the valley and the next valley,
between the hard earth and the black sky,
at the moment when the moon stops spinning

silently and emits a thin note of joy,
at the moment a bird suddenly sings
in the night, you are pierced

through both eyes with pine needles.
There is no blood, only a thin streak
of silver as you run on, seeing

as clearly as ever, moving forward
into a dark valley, descending the needle,
seeing with eyes all over your body.

◆   ◆   ◆

Calypso's Island

Animals always lead the way
into the earth. Down, down,
wolves lead the women,
down to the cave-heart,
back to their origin.

It has always been so
on this island of caves:
Animals lead the way,
women follow, becoming
animals and holy.

Into the black water go
the seal-women. Into
the cliff winds go the birds.
The horse-women rear.
They have fled beyond words.

This is the dream of the women
sleeping in the rock, hair
disheveled, breasts bare.
This is the dream of the women
in towns, in cities, everywhere.

◆　◆　◆

Litany of Earth

Beaver and gopher,
> *Cattle and kine.*

Badger and fox,
> *Camel and swine.*

Antelope, jackrabbit,
> *Rabbit and lamb.*

Walrus and muskox,
> *Nanny and ram.*

Marmot and chipmunk,
> *Cattle and kine.*

Weasel and mink,
> *Camel and swine.*

Bobcat and jaguar,
> *Rabbit and lamb.*

Coyote and lynx,
> *Nanny and ram.*

Caribou, grizzly,
> *Cattle and kine.*

Pronghorn and moose,
> *Camel and swine.*

Skunk, armadillo,
> *Rabbit and lamb.*

'Possum and mouse.
> *Nanny and ram.*

Sea lion, otter,
  Cattle and kine.
Mountain goat, mole,
  Camel and swine.
Puma and ocelot,

  Rabbit and lamb.
Porcupine, vole.
  Nanny and ram.

Elk, deer, and antelope,
  Cattle and kine.
Prairie dog, hare,
  Camel and swine.
Mule deer and marten,
  Rabbit and lamb.
Wolverine, bear,
  Nanny and ram.

◆   ◆   ◆

Night

A great black cloak around my shoulders, all shadowy comfort.

Shapes dissolving into each other.

Enormity of small things: the movement of a clock's hand, the stirring of a curtain in a breeze, a timber creaking.

Someone breathing.

The space between silences.

I walk through the sleeping house, half wakeful, half in dream. I stand by the dark window, looking at the garden sleeping under snow. I feel the past write itself on the dim walls. I see the future cloud the sky.

I have no shape, no outline.

The most peace I know: not feelingless monotony, not bliss-ignorance, not blind hope, but standing in this certain place and time, feeling my shadow etch itself on the glass, knowing there will be others afterwards who sense my distant presence, knowing I am charged with the passions of those who went before. All their shadows fall upon the glass, forming the shape of my body.

I could reach through the glass. I could walk through the glass. In an instant, I would be in light. I would be light.

I could do that.

But this night, I stay in shadow. Comforting shades, presence, peace.

The silence between spaces.

The enormity of small things.

♦   ♦   ♦

Thief at the Wedding

Someone has stolen my veil.
I sit on the stone outside
the bright hall and weep.

I cannot be wed! A man wants
a woman whose wild hair
and wild eyes are hidden.

His rules cut like weapons
into my soft flesh. His rules
shroud me in dark mist.

I thought I would find safety
beneath that veil. I thought I
would finally be tamed. But now

the celebrants depart. The moon
sets. I rise. And I dance, my hair
wild and silver, while my thief watches.

◆　　◆　　◆

Maeve's Complaint

There was a time
the friendship
of my upper thighs
drove men to war.

There was a time
my sun-bright hair
struck men blind, oh
there was a time—

Oh damn such talk.
Memories are nothing
to the heat of a hand
on a willing thigh, and

all the lovers I have had
—so many, oh so many—
are nothing to me now
as I lie here alone—

All that I have ever been
I am now, I am richer
and riper and warmer
than the girl I once was,

oh I know things now
that girl never dreamed,
ways to please and be pleased,
that only age knows,

but damn! I'm alone
while the simplest girl
with a crooked smile
has a man in her bed.

I have power and gold
enough for two men.
I can buy or command
whatever I want.

Except this. Except love.
Hot blood never cools.
I'm the same as I was.
Oh damn! To be young!

♦ ♦ ♦

The Maenad Remembers Dionysus

Where have I seen you, boy?
Once on a dock, sea wind
wetting your face. Once in a field,
grass brushing your cheek. Once
standing in a forest like a new pine.

I have seen you rarely but I did
not know how rare, how scarce
you were. You seemed forever
nearby. Now I know you to be
northern lights, meteor showers,

mostly absent. I know that I will die
in your absence. There will be one time
that is the last time and I will not
know it. I will not know it until later.
And that is my sorrow. That is my joy.

♦　♦　♦

The Hag of Beare Sings to Her Lover

That time in a ring of grass,
when I thought you were
the sky. That other time,
dawn haloing your hair.
That time when you were
dark wine, hot on my lips.

Now you are gray and thin.
I am graying and not thin.
I stumble on my words,
you talk too much too fast,
we are jumpy and abrupt
as though we have just met.

So many years to make some
sense of love, and we are no
nearer. But we know something,
dear heart, despite the years
and distances between us.
And what is that? Ah, ah,

as you would say. Ah, ah. Words
fail. There is no name for what
we are, for what we know of love
and of each other. We pass like comets
through each other's lives, leaving no trace
except brief rituals of arrival and departure.

So let us celebrate those rituals again,
my dear, for time grows short and dangerous,
my love, my ancient friend, and one day
there will be no trace of any of those times
we spent, though other lovers will come
to stumble wondering and wonderingly in our wake.

◆   ◆   ◆

Procedure for Reclaiming the Self

she presses eyes and
remembers sight and

touches temples and
remembers blood and

twists her hair and
recalls that

thought
is space

in the hands of a lover she
forgets herself yes

I forget myself
I had forgotten

the outlines of this solitude
this body etched on air

once and transitory, more
lasting than leaves, more

temporary than trees, fleet
compared to stones

now remembering its
edges, its dissolutions

I come back
I always must

come back
this distance

far from you
far into

my wildnesses
my own oceans

my glacial
splendors

my mountain
silences

my vast
interior plains

♦   ♦   ♦

Vigil at the Well

A rock ledge. A dark pool.
Pale dawn and cold rain.

And a woman alone
holding three coins.

She circles the well
three times in the rain.

She offers the coins
to a great ancient tree

then bends to the pool.
A glimmer of silver.

Dawn striking the pool?
A fish in its depths?

The pool stills again.
The sky blazes red.

The woman gets up.
Nothing seems changed.

But the next day a wind
blows warm from the sea.

♦   ♦   ♦

Medusa in Winter

sisters press me with your
shoulders, I grow cold this
night, this dark day

rest with me, night
cannot end if
thigh does not press
thigh and breasts
nest in no hollow

our hair twists
into sleep, my face
twists against the night
and my wings ache

sisters, mirrors
should I die before
this winter-sleep
relaxes you awake

fear not
steeds pound my
dreams, winged
stallions free from
death, fear not

magnificence rides
in me—it will
spring

♦   ♦   ♦

Burials

What if, a millennium from now, you
are exhumed dressed completely in gold,
every limb, every finger circled with sun
metal twisted into snakes and flowers?

What if they find you wrapped in a shroud
of silver meshed like spider webs? Or covered
with a boulder big as yourself? Or beheaded,
your skull set in a niche to hold candles,
a sconce behind you like a halo?

What if they find that you were burned, and
traces of the ceremony show it was at dusk,
and that you rode a chariot or a boat
into the afterlife? Or if they find threads
of a cocoon that held you, the only thing except
your bones to survive so long? If so, what

would they say? This is the body of a woman
hale but bent with age, this is the body
of a woman who bore many children,
this is the body of a woman who lost
several teeth, this is the body of a woman
who lived on chestnuts and occasional lambs' meat?

This is the body of a woman,
they would say, and
from a millennium of death
how could you say back:

Not just a young girl dead in childbirth but
a woman blasted from the impact of creation,
not just a woman in her prime but
a mother of the tribe, not just
an old woman but a hallowed elder,
not a woman but a priest,
not a woman but a queen,
not a woman but a vessel for
the energy of goddess?

This is what they hide from us:
Forty thousand years ago a crone was buried
nested in the arms of her young lover
who killed himself upon her death.

Behold, behold.

♦   ♦   ♦

EPILOGUE

Drawing Down the Goddess

She is the drum.
The skin on which life plays.
The pulse. The pounding heart.
Rhythm of starlight and blood.
The rap, the tap, the roll,
the clap, the rattle, the thunder.
Foot to ground, hand to hand.
Our hearts drum. And drum.
She is the drum.

Return to her.
Return to yourself.

She is the voice.
Voice before words.
Cry of hunger. Cry of need.
Sob of fear. Hiss of pain.
Voice beyond words.
Satisfaction's murmur. Shouts of joy.
Panting urgency of sex.
Animals, birds, whales, women, men,
clanging and chiming, silvery and hoarse,
sweet and clear and loud and strong.
She is the voice.

The hour has arrived:
Invoke her now.

She is the wind.
Tender breeze of spring
under a breathless moon.
Summer's exhalation,
that warm green sigh.
Fall squalls, tempests of death
under a hunter moon.
The howling winter storm.
Fluting, piping, whistling, wind
through our bodies, trumpeting,
bugling, wind through our bodies.
She is the wind.

Reach in and touch her.
Call out and hear her.

She is the dance.
Frenzy of hips and thighs,
hot desire oceans,
dark need and brightest joy.
Breasts pressing air.
Arms reaching, hands meeting,
heads swaying, eyes closing.
She is the dancer.
She is the dance.

Return to her.
Return to yourself.

She is the drum, the voice,
the wind, the dance and
beyond words and time,
beyond knowing and the known,
beyond body and spirit moving through body,
beyond song and the singer,
beyond drums and the drummer,
beyond dance and the dancer,
she is the silence.

The hour has arrived:
Invoke her now.

Reach in and touch her.
Call out and hear her.

Return to her.
Return to yourself.

♦   ♦   ♦

Notes

Warning

In many lands, it is believed that witches sneakily cast spells by using the discarded fingernails, toenails, hair, even flakes of skin, of their victims. According to the theory of sympathetic magic, part equals whole. So burnt hair would cause the person from which it was cut to feel the pain of fire, throwing hair into water would result in drowning (or perhaps pneumonia, drowning in one's own fluids), and so forth. It is also frequently believed that women, if they had power, would abuse it as readily as men have. If this is true, one should be especially wary of women barbers and dentists.

Hera Renews Her Youth

The Hera of this book is not the nasty Olympian queen known for her jealous rages; that goddess was a diminution of the earlier, pre-Hellenic cow goddess who represented women in all the ages of their lives. The original Hera was honored in the Heraion, precursor to the Olympic Games, in which women ran in age-ranked groupings to acknowledge the three ages of the goddess. The young Hera, called Hebe or Green Hera, was honored with rituals in which her statue was renewed with a bath in a nearby river, new clothing, and the celebrations of her followers.

The Goddess Instruction Manual, Part I: How to Think like Athena

The goddess Athena appears in Greek literature as a motherless warrior whose loyalty is to the masculine force. But that goddess descends from an earlier one, a motherly protector of the household and family. In the same way that the classical Athena was severed from her femininity, thought today is imagined as somehow separate from the body, a fallacy that has led to many social and interpersonal woes.

Maia, Grandmother Spring

The Roman goddess after whom our month of May is named was both a nymph and a grandmother. Many ancient cultures saw life as cyclical, not linear, and thus the crone who turns into a maiden is a common motif in mythology and folklore.

Wild Sound

The title comes from a term used by filmmakers to describe ambient sound, the almost-inaudible sound that surrounds us but to which we usually do not attend. Between people, too, there is a kind of wild sound, inarticulated needs and desires that form a background to our lives together. Such desires can create monumental change, for which we may be unprepared if we have muffled our awareness.

She Who Watches and Holds Still

Most poems in this book are based in folklore or mythology but some, like this one, emerged from the dreams of the poet. Many cultures believe that dreams are not just bizarre combinations of images brought on by eating pickles too close to bedtime, but are messages from our deeper selves. Dreams usually cloak their messages in stories such as this one, which describes a moment of readiness for inevitable change.

Altar of the East

Spring is usually associated with the east, the place of the sun's daily birth. Both spring and dawn are times of fresh potential. Babies, buds, bunnies, and similar young beings are common images for spring. East is also associated with air, and by extension with birds, the beings of air. Birds in turn are a common symbol for spring, because of their mating and nest-building activities in that season.

Aubade for Aurora: Her Lover Sings to the Dawn Goddess

Goddesses of dawn, found in many cultures, are notoriously promiscuous, possibly because dawn spreads her light indiscriminately. Aurora, the Roman dawn goddess after whom the dancing lights at the North and South Pole are named, was a supremely generous and wanton lover who was, however, as quick to leave as to come. Her partner here sings a song in the medieval tradition of the aubade or dawn song, in which each verse must end with the word "dawn."

Litany of Air

Litanies—quite simply, lists—are an important liturgical form that catalogues important religious material: saints' names, titles of the deity, and so forth. In a time and a land when children recognize five hundred times more brand names than names of natural beings, it is important that we begin once again to know our neighbors on this earth. Spring is associated with the east, which is in turn associated with the element of air; thus it is appropriate that the names of birds be sung out in springtime.

Venus of Lespugue

The "Venuses" of ancient Europe were carved between 24,000–27,000 years ago and attest to the worship of a primary feminine divinity. Because the people who honored her lived so long before written history began, we do not know the name her original worshippers gave to the goddesses carved from ivory and bone; they are named for the towns in which archaeologists unearthed them. One of the famous goddesses of Paleolithic Europe, the Venus found in Lespugue has an arched neck and bulbous breasts; she seems to be part bird.

Swan Maiden

In European folklore, probably based on ancient tribal religions, the goddess appears in the form of a young woman who wears a swan's garment but who takes it off occasionally to bathe. At such times she may be captured by anyone who would steal her garments and hide them. The beautiful creature would then be trapped in human form and, although she might marry and bear children, would feel imprisoned and mournful. Should she find the missing garment, she would put it on and fly away—no matter how much love she bore for her human family.

Finola's Song

One of the most famous swan maidens was the daughter of the Irish King Lir, Finola, who was cursed by her evil stepmother to spend 900 years in the form of a swan. Her younger brothers were changed at the same time, and so Finola spent almost a full millennium caring for them in storms and fine weather. When they finally returned to human form, all the years they had lived suddenly passed over them and they disappeared in whirlwinds of dust.

The Fool

The tarot deck, sometimes used as a fortunetelling tool, is an ancient series of symbolic pictures that permit the unconscious to bring its wisdom into waking life. The first card of the deck is the Fool, who appears in the conventional playing card deck as the Joker. Opportunities abound for the Fool (and those who draw the Fool)—but opportunities can lead to disaster as well as to success.

Nimue's Charm for Finding Love

One of the great sorceresses of Arthurian tradition, Nimue (also called Vivianne) took as her lover the great magician Merlin. This poem imagines her casting a spell to bring him to her. She uses a standard verse form called the charm, in which repeating words were thought to create a tight, inescapable circle around the person being enchanted.

Diana to Her Maiden

The Roman sky goddess Diana hunted through the forest with her band of nymphs. They refused any connection with the company of men; in fact, intrusive men were put to death by the goddess. In sculpture, Diana is often shown accompanied by hunting hounds, one of her emblems and an indication of her status as "Mistress of Beasts."

Atalanta to Her Father

In Greek legend, the Amazon Atalanta refused to marry anyone whom she could outrun. She was so speedy, however, that it was necessary to trick her into losing; the hero Meleager finally won a race with

Atalanta by distracting her with golden apples thrown in her path. Stooping to pick them up, she lost the race—but only by a fraction of a second.

Persephone's Invitation

The Greek spring maiden Persephone used to play with her maiden friends in the fragrant meadows of her mother, Demeter the earth goddess, until she was captured and taken to the underworld by its king Hades.

Persephone's Journey

In the most frequently told version of the myth of Persephone, the young goddess was abducted from the earth's surface by Hades, king of the underworld. For six months, her mother Demeter mourned, and the earth went into winter sadness. Persephone was found, but because she had eaten pomegranate seeds while in Hades' realm, she was thereafter his wife for six months of the year. This poem relies on other versions of the myth that show Persephone as more active in her courtship.

Fand Calls the Wild Hunt

The Irish imagined that there was a world parallel to our own, occupied by powerful and lovely beings who could be either helpful or destructive to humans. One of their leaders was the fairy queen Fand, who could be seen sometimes at the head of the Wild Hunt, a procession of mounted fairies who flew through the air, stealing children and lovers from this realm.

Maenad in Spring

The maenads practiced a woman's religion in Greece in approximately the sixth century B.C.E. Women left their homes and families to spend their nights in nearby forests and mountains. Because their religion was kept secret, we have no way of knowing what they did when they answered the call of their god, Dionysus, but it is assumed that their rites were ecstatic, as were the Celtic Mayday festivals traditionally celebrated with hilltop fires.

Maeve Prepares for Beltane

One of the greatest goddesses of ancient Ireland was Maeve. She was the ruler of the land's abundance, whose consort became king when he sipped from her cup of sacred red mead. It was important for Maeve to be the equal of her partner in all ways, and she was willing to fight to ensure her equality. Here she prepares for the sacred spring feast of Beltane by connecting with her own inner sovereignty.

On Mayday Eve

The Celtic feast of Beltane or Mayday Eve was once celebrated with sexual rituals, perhaps involving anonymous matings in the woodlands.

As on the opposite feast of Samhain (Halloween), the door to the other world was open on this night, permitting visitations from beyond.

Hera Celebrates Her Ripeness

In her second phase, Hera, the Great Goddess of Greece, was called Hera Telia, "the Perfect One." At this point in her endlessly regenerating cycle, Hera welcomed the opportunity to mate and to form relationships. It is apparently this phase of Hera that was debased into the jealous goddess known to classical mythology.

Deirdre's Pledge to Her Lover

One of the great romantic legends of Ireland revolves around the young woman Deirdre of the Sorrows. Chosen to wed a king, Deirdre knew her own heart and escaped with her true love into the wilderness. But Deirdre and her lover were tricked into returning, whereupon he was put to death. Rather than be forced into marriage with her lover's murderer, Deirdre killed herself.

Instructions

Another dream-poem. In some lands, dreams were not to be interpreted but expressed. Someone who dreams of a special garment must make and wear it; someone who dreams of a dance or ritual must perform it. Similarly, some dreams call out to be written into poems.

Dame Gothel's Love for Rapunzel

Dame Gothel is the name given to the old woman who, when she found Rapunzel's father stealing her onions, demanded the man's first-born child. Delivered in young adulthood, golden-haired Rapunzel was so beautiful that Dame Gothel confined her at the top of a high tower. Although usually reviled by storytellers, it is possible that Dame Gothel truly loved Rapunzel, as this poem suggests.

The Goddess Instruction Manual, Part Two: How to Act like a Maenad

Thousands of women, perhaps hundreds of thousands, joined in the ecstatic rituals of the ancient maenads of Greece. But not a single one of them ever revealed the form of their secret worship. It is believed to have been ecstatic, but how the women attained that ecstacy is unknown.

The Maps of Magic

Tribal people worldwide know that trees require frequent offerings. In North America, tobacco is a traditional gift. In Ireland, trees frequently enjoy having white paper or cloth called clooties tied, ribbonlike, to their branches. In general, we have forgotten to honor the great trees among whom we live. Our world is not a better place for that forgetting.

The Forest Rules

The planet is not ours to control and use as we will. The forest, the desert, the oceanside: all have their own unique laws, known to us as the science of ecology. Reading the rules of the land is a skill known to many ancient peoples but mostly lost today.

Wisdom of Elders

The word "elder" has two meanings: a wise older person and a tree of great mythic importance. Just as our human elders tell us secrets from their long lives, the trees have their own deep wisdom to impart. Part of that wisdom is that they are not isolated beings but are connected to the life around them.

Venus of Willendorf

The Willendorf goddess is a tiny but massive-appearing sculpture of a rotund woman with full breasts. She is one of the oldest and most revered images of the mother goddess, carved somewhere in central Europe early in the Paleolithic or Old Stone Age, some 30,000 years ago.

Transit of Venus

In astrology, when a planet transits or passes in orbit over other planets, its energy is believed to alter theirs. In this poem, the feminine planet Venus is transiting over the other major planets. Although it is often said that Venus rules sensuality and passivity, those culture-laden interpretations of femininity do not explain the true effects of woman's power, which the world is experiencing in this vision. Doves are a traditional symbol of the goddess of lust.

Maeve in Summer

The Irish Maeve married the king, for she was the land, made fertile by her chosen consort. The inauguration of the Irish king involved drinking from the cup of red-gold mead that Maeve (whose name means "intoxication") offered him. So long as the king was righteous, Maeve would cause the land to be fertile and the people to be prosperous. But should the king be ungenerous or otherwise evil, Maeve withheld the crops until he was replaced.

Cybele's Song

Cybele, the goddess of the Anatolian peninsula (now Turkey), won many converts in the multicultural city that was ancient Rome, to which the huge black stone that represented her was carried after a prophecy that it would keep the city safe. Cybele was portrayed as a matronly woman surrounded by lions and bearing a sun-shaped drum.

Strength

In the tarot's major arcana, Strength is depicted as a woman of fairly delicate stature restraining an immense and powerful lion. This poem is a classic sonnet, one of the strongest verse forms.

Altar of the South

The direction of the sun at noon from the Northern Hemisphere, south is as a result connected with the element of fire. Fire in turn represents passion: not sexual passion alone, but also the passion of creativity in all its forms.

The Divine Sons Praise Saule
As She Dances on the Hilltop

Among the world's most charming folksongs are the hundreds of thousands that praise the goddesses of Lithuania and Latvia. Among those riches, the most lovely are the songs in praise of the sun, Saule, the mother who dances in silver shoes each summer solstice and cares for all her earthly children with dedication and joy. The Divine Sons are twin gods of the Balts, an ancient people who settled along the sea that bears their name.

The Buck at Noontime

The Celtic god Cernunnos often appeared with stag horns, for his name means simply "the horned one." A divinity of the Earth, he incarnated the mystery of life, death, and reproduction. This poem records an encounter with a majestic stag in the forests of Ireland's County Monaghan, on the estate at Annaghmakerrig—a stag that bore the energy of the ancient Horned One into the present.

Fire-Feast

The Celtic firefeast of Lughnasa (Lammas) was held on August 1 to celebrate the harvest and to mourn the dying of summer's light. It was a celebration of the unity of the community, a time when contracts were to be made and trial marriages contracted. Games and contests of strength pitted the young men against each other, no doubt to the delight of the young women. Some of the modern men in this poem have embodied the Celtic god Cernunnos, while others lose that opportunity through fear or timidity.

Litany of Fire

It may seem morbid to list the names of trees in a litany to fire. Yet fire, far from being the enemy of the forest, exists in a complex relationship to its trees and brush. Some species actually require fire to germinate; others, like the burr oak of the American savannahs, grow stronger as fire clears out competing underbrush. Trying to banish fire, so much a natural part of the ecosytem, from forests has led in recent years to massive accumulation of dead trees that resulted in some of the worst fires in history.

Freya's Love Charm

The Scandinavian love goddess Freya was connected with the fertility of the summer fields, especially fields of grain, which were said to resemble her lovely golden hair. The repetitive charm form captures her intended and holds him in her power.

Garland Sunday, and She Calls Her Lover to Join Her on the Mountain

Garland Sunday is one of the many names given in Ireland to the old Celtic feast of Lughnasa, festival of the sun's passage through the long productive summer season and into the time of its decline. In the West of Ireland, the holiday was celebrated by climbing tall mountains to harvest and eat fresh berries.

Praisesong for Her

The poem is based on the song of Amergin, Ireland's first poet, who claimed an ability to shapeshift into many forms. The goddess, too, takes many forms, including those mentioned here. The poem is in triplets, honoring the goddess's three forms and the ancient Celtic poetic triad. The line "I am a tear of the sun" appears in the original; its meaning is still undetermined.

Hera Alone, on the Mountain

Traditionally, the Greek Hera had three forms: as Hebe the Nymph, Hera the Perfect, and the Widow. But we count four seasons, although there is nothing magical in that number, and other cultures have counted two, three, and five seasons. This poem offers a second, later view of Hera the Perfect; as she approaches her annual retreat from life into widowhood, Hera looks both forward to solitude and back to her lavish summer energies. The poem is in the form of a chiasmus, each verse rhyming out from a center line.

The Star

This card in the tarot's major arcana shows a woman stepping into a pool of water while emptying a vessel; the star of the card's name shines overhead. Usually the image is interpreted as representing idealism and hopeful dreams.

Litany of Water

The direction of west is associated with fall and, in turn, with the element of water. And water, in turn, is connected to the emotions and to the unconscious, which often speaks to us through our emotions. Thus the fish that swim in the world's oceans and fresh waters are symbols of human feeling as well as of the ability to dive into emotional depths.

Edain's Charm for Lasting Love

If ever there was a goddess who knew about how to make love last, it was the Irish goddess Edain (also spelled Etain). She loved and was loved by the fairy king Midir, who was unfortunately already involved with another woman, a sorceress who cast a spell on Edain so that she was transformed into one creature after another until, at last, she became a bug. In that form she fell into a glass of ale and was drunk down by a princess, who gave birth to the reborn Edain, who grew up to become queen. But Midir came calling and kissed her. Immediately her memory of their love returned and, transformed into swans, they flew away together.

Pomona Sings to the Old Woman

Pomona, Roman goddess of autumn, represented the fruitful harvest. Once, it was told, she was courted by all the gods, but refused them to pursue an old woman, who later turned out to be the fertility god Vertumnus in disguise.

The Goddess Instruction Manual, Part Three: How to Make Love like Oshun

In Africa, Oshun was a water goddess whose body was the river that bears her name. With her people, she migrated to the New World, where she continues to be honored as a feminine essence of love.

Maeve's Discourse on Beauty

The great queen and goddess Maeve was nothing if not lustful; she is described in one great poem as offering a man "the friendship of her upper thighs" and claims she "never had one man without another in his shadow." Such a woman would certainly have enjoyed male beauty. This poem is inspired by an eighth-century Irish poem in which Maeve's daughter Findabhair—Maeve in maiden form—describes her lover Froech.

Venus of Laussel

A bas-relief in which a fleshy, faceless woman holds an empty cornucopia marked with lines, the Paleolithic Venus of Laussel is from an era when women apparently marked their menses on bone calendars.

Altar of the West

The west is the direction of the setting sun, and therefore is readily associated with evening and with the mysteries of the otherworld. In Irish mythology, the enchanted Land of Youth lies to the west, somewhere in the ocean on an island that drifts rather than remaining in one place.

Caer's Song to Her Beloved

The Irish goddess Caer was the beloved of Aengus, god of poetry. She came to him in haunting dreams until he set out in search of her. He found her swimming on a magical lake with her maidens, all of them connected by a golden chain. Transforming himself into a swan as well, Aengus joined her to fly happily away.

Housemagic
According to chaos theory, we cannot be certain of the causes of weather or other natural phenomenon, for according to the theory of sensitive dependence upon initial conditions, even the smallest motion can set into motion major changes. Dream theory suggests that we participate in archetypal reality in everyday life. A woman's home can be seen as a center of magical connection with all the world.

Amulets and Talismans

Throughout the world, people have believed that wearing or displaying significant objects both warded off evil (amulets) and attracted good luck (talismans). Even though today many people claim to have left such folkways behind, almost everyone dresses and decorates symbolically, if often unconsciously.

The Witch Threatened
Many cultures have believed that, because like attracts like, knots could tie up an enemy, and knives or open scissors could cut their energy (as well as their fingers). Knowing the name of one's attacker was considered important to forestall or untangle such bad magic. Let us hope our witch learns that name soon.

The Witch Complains of Hansel
One of the most famous stories collected by the Grimm brothers in rural Germany was that of a wicked witch who lived in the woods and ate children. The story is invariably told from the children's point of view. But maybe Hansel was not just a victim after all. Or is the witch just finding an excuse for what she plans to do anyway?

She Hexes Newscasters
There is no proof that blue candles are effective in stopping horrific news reports. There is, however, also no proof they are not.

She Visits the Trollwife
There are entities even more powerful than witches. The trollwife is an eastern European boogey-woman who lived on the edge of the wilderness, in the liminal space between human and nonhuman. She has a thing or two to teach even our witch-heroine.

The Measure of Her Powers
Magic is not just a matter of getting your own way. It means falling into a new relationship with the world, which may well demand something back from you for what it gives. If you do not answer those demands, beware.

Night of the Black Mirror

The Celtic feast of Samhain is today's Halloween, having lost little of its original meaning as a day when the veils between this world and the next are lifted, permitting visitations from beyond. Traditional games on this date, like bobbing for apples, crystal gazing, and cutting cakes that had a single nut in them, were originally divinations that revealed which of the Halloween celebrants would not live through the winter. Those whose fate was thus sealed—for what was foretold on this night could not be avoided—were granted a period of foreknowledge of death in which to settle their affairs.

A Vision of Hunger in Flesh

Communion means eating, as well as eating together. In the great game of life and death, hunter and prey are joined and ultimately become one being, which then is devoured by yet another.

In His Last Moments, Oisin Praises Niamh of the Golden Hair

The Irish poet Oisin was stolen away from human life by a beautiful fairy queen with whom he lived very happily in an island in the west. But he grew homesick and, against Niamh's strong warning, went back to the land of mortals. But fairy time is different than ours; those few months with Niamh were actually hundreds of years. The moment he set foot on earthly soil, Oisin felt all his years come upon him. Within a few moments, he withered, died, and became dust. But Niamh, he tells us, was worth it all. The poem is in the traditional Gaelic triad form.

The Old Song of the Tribes

To many peoples, death was not an ending but the beginning of a new adventure. This often included rebirth in a new body—reincarnation, becoming incarnate again. Many of those who believe in such rebirth also believe that those we love in one lifetime will come back to bring us joy—and pain—once again in the next.

Hera Celebrates Her Solitude

In her final, third stage, the great goddess Hera was called Theia, the woman alone. Annually, the goddess retreated from everyone, including her worshippers, to live alone in the wilderness. This retreat was celebrated by the Greeks of the city-state of Argos once a year when they left Hera's statue in the forest overnight, then reclaimed it, redressed it, and showed her forth, reborn as Hebe.

Angerona, Signaling Silence

In the Temple of Winter in Rome, a veiled statue with finger to lips was honored at the winter solstice. Little else is known of Angerona.

Ishtar, Ishtar

Goddess of sexual love in the Eastern Mediterranean, Ishtar was said to have been honored in rituals in which sexuality was celebrated by matings between people who did not disclose their names to each other.

Journey to the Mountains of the Hag

In the west of Ireland, in east County Clare, stretches a line of low mountains called Slieve Echghte, the Mountains of the Hag. These mountains are near the Atlantic Ocean and the famous Cliffs of Moher, with the sheer rocky fall called Hag's Head. Nestled in the mountains is a quiet place called Lough Graney, the Sun Maiden's Lake. This poem records a winter solstice journey to Lough Graney.

The World

The tarot's major arcana ends with the card called the World, which indicates that a cycle has been completed and a new one is about to begin. While considered a happy omen, it also indicates that new challenges lie ahead.

Omens

There are several times during the solar year that people have traditionally sought omens, symbolic indications of what is to come. Winter solstice is one of those traditional times. Many cultures have offered information, sometimes complex, about how to determine if an omen has been received and how to interpret it.

The Goddess Instruction Manual, Part Four: How to Dance with Kali

Kali, the goddess of death in Hindu India, is embraced as a mother by her worshippers. Many cultures have seen death this way, as a feminine force that is not threatening but natural. Kali is seen in much Hindu art as a dancer, inviting us to join her in that inevitable dance.

Sheila-na-Gig

Like the Paleolithic Venuses from the continent, the Irish figure called Sheila-na-Gig is an ancient one. It portrays a skeletal woman with bulging eyes and a wild grin, who holds open her vulva. She is a life-in-death or death-in-life figure whose origins are lost in prehistory.

Death Cammas

Herbal doctors and midwives knew the secrets not only of healing plants but of those that could assist a patient in a transition to the next life. Gathering these dangerous plants was commonly hedged about with complicated magical formulae.

Snow White on the Apple
The fairy tale has it that Snow White was tricked into eating the apple that put her into a profound sleep, to be awakened only by her true love. But perhaps Snow White saw it another way.

Altar of the North
The direction of north is associated with earth and with the body. It is the winter direction, from which the sun retreats in its annual cycle. As such, it is also associated with darkness, hibernation, and hidden growth.

Seeing Through the Flesh Eye
The idea that the senses are restricted to one organ is a relatively rare one. Many cultures have thought it possible to see without using the eye, as it was thought possible to hear without using the ears. Shamanic states of consciousness may have been necessary for such expanded senses.

Calypso's Island
Gozo is a tiny island off Malta that is called, by tradition, the home of the nymph Calypso. Appearing in the *Odyssey* as Ulysses' savior, she may have been a powerful pre-Greek goddess. On the main isle of Malta, dozens of temples to the goddess stand, the oldest extant human buildings. In the underground Hypogeum there, priestesses are believed to have slept, perhaps surrounded by snakes, to gain transformation.

Litany of Earth
The element of earth is connected with the powers of animals, both wild and domesticated. This litany honors both, for their own strength and beauty and for what they bring to the world.

Thief at the Wedding
In cultures where women are not free, complex regulations often attend upon such life passages as marriages, and women are rejected by society should anything inappropriate occur, even if they are unable to prevent it. Women forced to live on the margins of society suffer but are also freer than those who accept its rules.

Maeve's Complaint
Haughty, lusty Maeve was never described in ancient Irish literature as anything but young and strong. But she must have aged like any woman. And like any woman, she remained herself in age: fierce and feisty.

The Maenad Remembers Dionysus

The religion of Dionysus in ancient Greece was entirely a women's religion. Women left home and hearth to wander on the mountains together, celebrating secret rituals.

The Hag of Beare Sings to Her Lover

In Irish, her name is Cailleach, "the veiled one." She is one of the oldest goddesses of Ireland, probably reaching back to the pre-Celtic period. In historical literature she appears as a woman who grows young every time she meets a man who interests her. But this poem is based upon the famous "Lament of the Hag Beare" in which she speaks longingly of her youth.

Procedure for Reclaiming the Self

Most love spells focus on the love object rather than the lover. Similarly, most spells work only to draw lovers together. Yet unless a lover can be apart from the beloved, the love spell is only partial. This spell balances intense connection with a lover with intense connection with the self.

Vigil at the Well

Across Ireland on February 1, people still go to holy wells, sites sacred to the goddess that have been rededicated to saints. The feast and the wells are both dedicated to Saint Brigid, who was herself converted from being a Celtic goddess of fire, prophecy, and healing, whose festival, called Imbolc, was celebrated on the same day as the saint's feast. Seeing a fish in one of the holy wells is considered especially propitious.

Medusa in Winter

Medusa was one of three Gorgon sisters, all winged creatures who lived at the end of time. Athena set her hero Perseus to behead Medusa—which may have roots not in violence but in shamanic traditions of psychic dismemberment that leads to spiritual growth. The winged horse Pegasus leapt from the goddess's head as it was struck off by Athena's servant.

Burials

Archaeology is an inexact science; people are likely to interpret what they see through the lenses of their own lives and cultures. The skeleton of the old woman nestled in the arms of her young lover was found in the Grimaldi caves in Europe; they are from the early Neolithic or New Stone Age period, between 10,000 and 5,000 years ago.

Music on

Seasons of the Witch

1. *Warning*. Music, vocals, guitar, and harmony by Lili McGovern; lead guitar and bass by Mike Riopel.

Spring

2. *Altar of the East*. Music, vocals, piano, and keyboards by Claudia Blythe. 3. *Swan Maiden*. Music, vocals, and keyboards by Sally Coombs. 4. *Aubade for Aurora: Her Lover Sings to the Dawn Goddess*. Music and vocals by Claudia Blythe; cello by Helen Howarth; harmonies by Peggy Monaghan and Charlie Hewitt. 5. *Finola's Song*. Music and vocals by Kirsten Baird Gustafson; keyboards by Kathleen Bielawski; flute by Barbara Eberhart. 6. *On Mayday Eve*. Music and guitars by James Robbins; vocals by Peggy Monaghan; voiceover by Susan LaCroix. 7. *Maenad in Spring*. Music and guitar by James Robbins; vocals by Peggy Monaghan. 8. *Fand Calls the Wild Hunt*. Music, vocals, piano, and drums by Claudia Blythe. 9. *Maeve Prepares for Beltane*. Music, vocals, and guitar by Lili McGovern; lead guitar and bass by Mike Riopel; violin by Heather Adrian; harmonies by Peggy Monaghan.

Summer

10. *Altar of the South*. Music, vocals, and piano by Claudia Blythe. 11. *Hera Celebrates Her Ripeness*. Music and vocals by Peggy Monaghan; keyboards by Neal Harris. 12. *Cybele's Song*. Music by Susan LaCroix; vocals by Peggy Monaghan; piano by James Robbins. 13. *Praise Song for Her*. Music and vocals by Susan LaCroix.

Fall

14. *Altar of the West*. Music, vocals, and piano by Claudia Blythe. 15. *Amulets and Talismans*. Music by James Robbins and Peggy Monaghan; vocals by Peggy Monaghan; guitars by James Robbins. 16. *Night of the Black Mirror*. Music by James Robbins and Peggy Monaghan; vocals by Peggy Monaghan; keyboards by James Robbins. 17. *Caer's Song to Her Beloved*. Music, vocals, and guitar by Kirsten Baird Gustafson; flute by Barbara Eberhart; harmonies by Peggy Monaghan and Charlie Hewitt. 18. *A Vision of Hunger in Flesh*. Music and guitars by James Robbins; vocals by Peggy Monaghan. 19. *Mabon*. Music, vocals, and guitar by Lili McGovern; lead guitar and bass by Mike Riopel.

Winter

20. *Altar of the North*. Music, vocal, and piano by Claudia Blythe; drum by Peggy Monaghan. 21. *Snow White on the Apple*. Music and piano by James Robbins; vocals by Peggy Monaghan. 22. *Thief at the Wedding*. Music by James Robbins and Peggy Monaghan; vocals by Peggy Monaghan; guitars by James Robbins. 23. *The Maenad Remembers Dionysus*. Music and guitars by James Robbins; vocals by Peggy Monaghan. 24. *Procedure for Reclaiming the Self*. Music and guitars by James Robbins; vocals by Peggy Monaghan.

Spring

25. *Maenad in Spring (Reprise)*. Music, vocals, and keyboards by Sally Coombs.

◆   ◆   ◆

All lyrics are by Patricia Monaghan, from *Seasons of the Witch* (Llewellyn Publications, 2002). More information on Patricia Monaghan can be found on her website at:

www. patriciamonaghan.com

Special thanks to all those who supported this project in this and its previous incarnation, especially Tom Brooks, Mary Hewitt, Todd and Conor McGovern, Bill Blythe, Ken Sease, Amy Knapp, Diane McIntyre, and Kathleen Bielawski.

Recorded at Affinity Music (Marin County, California) and Mirror Studios (Anchorage, Alaska).

Engineered by Neal Harris and Charlie Hewitt.

Produced by Peggy Monaghan.

"Swan Maiden" and "Maenad In Spring (Reprise)" produced by Sally Coombs.

More information on Arctic Siren Records can be found at:

www. arcticsiren.com